CLASS LEADERS

Recovering a Tradition

David Lowes Watson

DISCIPLESHIP RESOURCES

MATERIALS FOR GROWTH IN CHRISTIAN FAITH AND LIFE

P.O. Box 189 • Nashville, TN 37202 • Phone (615) 340-7284

Cover design by Claudia Williams.

ISBN 0-88177-092-2

Library of Congress Card Catalog No. 90-82206

DR092B

In memory of
Richard Coates and H. Cecil Pawson

In recognition of
Ruth A. Coates and Polly W. Teagle

Contents

Acknowledgments

This book is published in the hope that it will quickly become out of date. If that does not happen, in large measure it will have failed in its intent. It is designed to assist in the revitalization of the office of class leader, one of Methodism's most distinctive traditions; and if this should take hold again in the church, growing numbers of laywomen and laymen will assume the office and give it powerful new dimensions. They will seize the reins of leadership in forming Christian disciples, and bring new authority to this vital and long-neglected work. As in the earliest days of Methodism, the pace set by such leaders will quickly outstrip any attempts to define their responsibilities on the written page. Let us hope, therefore, that only for the time being is a resource such as this required.

My first acknowledgment must be to the countless faithful Methodists across many generations who have nurtured strong lay leadership, most especially in the African American and Korean traditions of the church, where class leaders and class meetings were not allowed to die out. Some of these forebears and colleagues are acknowledged in the text of the book. Many more are nameless, quite simply because they were content to serve Christ without recognition.

The groundwork for the recovery of this tradition in The United Methodist Church has nowhere been laid more faithfully and thoroughly than in the hundreds of covenant discipleship groups that have been meeting for the past fifteen years throughout the United Strates, and in a number of other countries around the world. If the office of class leader resumes its proper place in the life and work of the congregation, these groups will have done much to establish its integrity. I remain personally and professionally grateful for this network of trusted colleagues. They are the essence of the people called Methodists.

I am further grateful for the collegiality of a number of senior United Methodist pastors who have seen the potential of covenant discipleship groups for congregational leadership, and have agreed to pilot class leaders for the connectional church: Brian K. Bauknight, Christ U.M.C., Bethel Park, Pennsylvania; Daniel T. Benedict, First U.M.C., Chula Vista, California; Dan E. Bonner, Jr., First U.M.C., Wichita, Kansas; Jim. K. Brown, Jr., Lake Highlands U.M.C., Dallas, Texas; Durward McCord, Belmont U.M.C., Nashville, Tennessee; and Robert R. Smith, Union U.M.C., Belleville, Illinois. These pastors and their congregations have served for some time as teaching centers for covenant discipleship, and they have both the vision and the experience to reintroduce class leaders to United Methodism. They are the vanguard of a new generation of Methodist leadership.

The nurturing of this intiative has been greatly facilitated by the professional freedom afforded by the General Board of Discipleship. The General Secretary, Ezra Earl Jones, fosters a collegial environment in which the Holy Spirit moves with breadth and power, and in which the rich diversity of the church is allowed wide expression. The administrative support of Victor Perez-Silvestry, Associate General Secretary, is always gracious and understanding. And my colleagues in the Office of Covenant Discipleship and Christian Formation, Phyllis Tyler-Wayman, Marigene Chamberlain, and Metral Smith, have assisted in this birth with skill, sensitivity, and constancy. I owe them a very great deal.

At Discipleship Resources, I am grateful for the insightful and supportive editing of Craig B. Gallaway, and the encouragement of David L. Hazlewood. My thanks are also due to J. Lee Bonnet for her creative production of the volume, and to Stephen L. Potter for his imaginative promotion of the entire project.

The book is dedicated to four class leaders, each of whom represents the best of the Methodist tradition, past and present. Richard Coates and Cecil Pawson touched countless lives for many years at Dilston Road and Hexham Road Methodist Churches in Newcastle upon Tyne, England. The harvest of their work is still being reaped. The leadership of Ruth Coates at Grace U.M.C., East St. Louis, Illinois, was a profound means of grace for me as a pastor, and for many others who belonged to her class over the years. Someone who learned to drive after retirement in order to gather and form Christian disciples will surely pass muster with the circuit riders when the final roll is called. The deep Christian wisdom of Polly Teagle is an enduring source of inspiration to the class she leads at Union U.M.C., Belleville, Illinois, to the General Board of Discipleship, where she serves as a Director, and to myself, through a friendship I have been privileged to enjoy for more than two decades.

These leaders, and the faithful company they represent, have answered a call to pastoral leadership just as surely as those of us who are ordained. Their credentials are impeccable. What remains is for the church once again to recognize their office.

General Board of Discipleship   May 1991
Nashville, Tennessee

Preface

*From the Explanatory Notes of Thomas Coke and
Francis Asbury in the 1798 Edition of the Doctrines and
Discipline of the Methodist Episcopal Church in America.*

CONCERNING CLASS LEADERS

The office is of vast consequence. The revival of
the work of God does perhaps depend as much
upon the whole body of leaders, as it does upon
the whole body of preachers.

For our leaders under God are the sinews of our
society, and our revivals will ever, in a great
measure, rise or fall with them.

Introduction

Recovering a Tradition

EVENTFUL LEGISLATION

In May 1988, the General Conference of The United Methodist Church, meeting in St. Louis, Missouri, took a significant step toward revitalizing the faithful discipleship that once was the mark of Methodism. Legislation was adopted restoring class meetings and class leaders to the *Book of Discipline*.[1]

Incorporated as paragraph 268, the legislation was drafted by Dr. Hae-Jong Kim, a Korean pastor who was then serving as a district superintendent in the Northern New Jersey Annual Conference. The church was not ready to go all the way with his proposal. The mandatory language of the original draft was amended to state that congregations *may* form class meetings and *may* appoint class leaders. But the legislation was eventful nonetheless. It addressed what many had long regarded as a serious weakening of United Methodist polity, namely, the decline of class leaders and class meetings. Indeed, since the uniting General Conference in 1939 of the Methodist Episcopal Church, the Methodist Episcopal Church, South, and the Methodist Protestant Church, they had ceased to have any disciplinary significance at all.[2]

THE GENIUS OF METHODISM

The irony of this decline is that class leaders and class meetings were the genius of the original Methodist movement. They were a highly effective means of pastoral nurture and oversight, first in John Wesley's early societies, and then in the family of Methodist churches throughout the world. The story of how they gradually lost their prominence, until their virtual omission from the 1939 *Discipline* was a mere formality, thus demands telling and re-telling—a task which remains a very open field for Methodist historians.

This is not to say that class leaders and class meetings disappeared from Methodism as a whole. The African American and Korean traditions in North America, to say nothing of other Methodist churches around the world, have continued to recognize their importance, and have retained them in their polity and practice. Even so, their restoration to the United Methodist *Book of Discipline* means that the mother church of Methodism, the church in direct succession to the Methodist Episcopal Church, has taken a momentous step toward recovering this most distinctive of all Methodist traditions: shared leadership of the church of Jesus Christ by clergy and laity, working together in creative Christian collegiality.

CLERGY AND CLASS LEADERS

As the title indicates, the focus of this volume will be the office of class leader and the ways in which it can foster the formation of Christian disciples. Accordingly, much of what follows is directed toward laypersons who sense a vocation to such leadership. There are chapters on discerning the call to become a class leader, on the nature and purpose of the office, on how to prepare for the tasks it involves, and on how to assume its responsibilities.

At the same time, pastors who read this book will find much that complements their role as ordained clergy. Hopefully, they will see that class leaders, by strengthening the pastoral oversight of the congregation, can free them to exercise the creative leadership they are called and trained to provide. This can only happen, of course, if clergy welcome class leaders as pastoral colleagues, and do not feel threatened by the vigor of their collegiality. It is important, therefore, to note that many of the early Methodist clergy started out as class leaders (see below, p. 40), as would doubtless be the case today had the office been retained in the life and work of the church. Class leaders provided strong collegiality for clergy then, and can do so again, because they both share a call to pastoral leadership.

The key to this early collegiality was mutual acknowledgment of vocation, and mutual recognition of gifts and graces. On the one hand, class leaders were not threatened by clergy. They knew that if they too should receive a call to ordination, this path was open to them, because so many class leaders had taken it. By the same token, clergy were not threatened by class leaders. They knew the importance of their leadership in the congregation, because so many of them had once held the office. Thus both were able to fulfill their respective vocations, and in so doing made Methodism one of the most powerful instruments for the coming reign of God this country has ever known.

Tragically, as we shall see, this rich collegiality was not sustained. But it lasted long enough to challenge us to recover it today. It will require the same mutual recognition and trust that were exercised by those early class leaders and circuit riders—collegial qualities that are very dependent on a Christ-centered approach to discipleship and congregational life. In addition to reading this book, therefore, class leaders and clergy should consult the companion volume, *Forming Christian Disciples*, where Christ-centeredness is discussed in some detail, with regard both to faithful discipleship and congregational vitality.

A FOCUS ON CLASS LEADERS

A further word needs to be said about our focus on the office of class leader, inasmuch as we shall have little to say about class meetings, even though the office and the institution have traditionally functioned together. This is in no way a disparagement of class meetings as a valid and vital means of Christian formation. On the contrary, in those branches of Methodism where class meetings have continued, their bonding and accountability remain a highly effective means of nurturing faithful disciples. However, there are several contextual factors impacting The United Methodist Church today that make it essential to revitalize the office of class leader before attempting any widespread reintroduction of class meetings.

The first is that church life in the United States is very much part of the North American culture. This is not the place to argue the benefits and drawbacks of such a social phenomenon, but merely to state it as a contextual reality. It means that people may belong to congregations, and may even attend worship on a regular basis, without a major adjustment to their lifestyle. Attending church is not an unusual activity. It rarely causes personal sacrifice, and it often brings marked social benefits.

This in turn means that many church members in the United States—in fact, the great majority—do not join congregations in order to be more accountable for their Christian living in the world. Nor do they regard it a condition of their church membership to meet weekly in a small group to check up on their discipleship. As we shall see in Chapter One, this can be viewed either as a handicap for the church, or as an opportunity for wider ministry and mission. But however it is viewed, we must accept that accountable discipleship is not a criterion of membership in the North American congregation of today. If we are to change this—and there is no doubt at all that it should be changed—we shall first need good leaders in discipleship.

The second factor is historical. In The United Methodist Church, the adult Sunday school class displaced the class meeting several generations ago as the primary means of Christian nurture. The change began in the last quarter of the nineteenth century, and it was very thorough. Instead of a weekly class meeting as a means of support and oversight for faithful discipleship, classes became a weekly time of instruction and discovery, albeit with important dynamics of fellowship. The principle of mutual accountability for living out one's discipleship gave way to personal exploration and fulfillment in company with like-minded friends and colleagues.

While the adult Sunday school is no longer what it once was, and while the Sunday school teachers many of us remember with gratitude and affection have largely been replaced with resources designed primarily for self-instruction, the Sunday school class nonetheless remains an important source of support and fellowship for a great many church members. Indeed, there are encouraging signs of its reinvigoration.[3] Thus, if class meetings were to be reintroduced as an integral feature of congregational life, in many instances they would be a programmatic redundancy. More important, the effort expended on their implementation would be a distraction from the most pressing need of the church today: the development of effective leadership in the forming of Christian disciples.

SMALL GROUPS

Yet another contextual factor making it imperative to begin with class leaders rather than class meetings is the contemporary fascination with small groups in much of North America. In a society impoverished by individualism and self-indulgence, they have become a basic tool in the forging of human relationships. Many people finding themselves in need of companionship or emotional support will often turn to organized small groups as a means of making new friends, or sharing mutual experiences, or avoiding loneliness—or even what sociologist Kurt Back has described as "the American middle class at play."[4]

To the extent that the church in the United States reflects this culture, and is often shaped by it, small groups play a similar role in a wide range of congregational activities. Many church members join such groups in order to meet their social needs rather than to apply themselves to the more important task of forming their discipleship. Indeed, the activities of some congregations are so culturally conditioned that the teachings of Jesus of Nazareth are the last thing many of their small groups place on their agenda.

Given this cultural conditioning, to attempt a recovery of class meetings without first revitalizing the office of class leader would risk them becoming merely another programmatic round of small groups. As such they would be measured, not by their formative value for Christian discipleship, but by the relational satisfaction they provided for their members—which in turn would place another administrative workload on pastoral staff.

THE HORSE BEFORE THE CART

The first step in recovering the Methodist tradition of accountable discipleship must therefore be the revitalization of class leaders, not class meetings. It may be that class meetings will one day be reinstated as a church-wide feature of Methodism; but not yet, and not through structural imposition. They must grow naturally and spontaneously out of the leadership of class leaders. To reintroduce class meetings in the North American church of today without first developing creditable leadership would be to ignore contextual reality. The horse must come before the cart.

COVENANT DISCIPLESHIP

This does not mean that the class meeting is entirely "on hold." In addition to those branches of Methodism where it has never been discontinued, it has been adapted for the contemporary church in the form of covenant discipleship groups. For the past fifteen years, these groups have been active throughout the United States and in a number of other countries around the world. The members meet for one hour each week, holding themselves mutually accountable for the basics of Christian living in the world (see the companion volume, *Covenant Discipleship*, DR091B).

Covenant discipleship, however, is not intended for the congregation as a whole. Usually no more than 15 percent of active church members participate, or some 5-7 percent of the membership roll. The groups are rather designed to develop leaders in discipleship, including class leaders. By no means everyone in a covenant discipleship group is a class leader; but all class leaders belong to such a group. By meeting week by week with others of like mind and purpose, to give an account of their discipleship, class leaders hold themselves responsible for precisely those areas of the Christian life where they exercise leadership. Just as important, they are *seen* to be accountable, and are thus able to lead by example.

If The United Methodist Church were to re-adopt the class meeting as a church-wide feature of membership, the mutual accountability of covenant discipleship groups would prove too demanding. The format would have to be more generally pastoral—something that tended to happen after Methodism became a church. These later class meetings were less rigorous than Wesley's original design; and, as we shall see in Chapter 3, their pastoral format gave the class leader an even more pivotal role than in Wesley's day. Significantly, this has also been the pattern in congregations where class leaders and class meetings have continued to function.

The priority therefore is clear. If we are to seek the formation of faithful Christian disciples, we must first recover the office of class leader. Class meetings may follow in due course, but our pressing need at present is for disciples to be formed by *example*. Such at least is the purpose of the chapters that follow, with the hope and prayer that they might help to recover this uniquely Methodist office, and provide some initial direction for the men and women who are called by God to accept its responsibilities.

AN ECHO OF THE CLASS LEADER

While there are branches of Methodism where class leaders still function, in most congregations they are only a memory. Yet sometimes the memory comes alive, as happened some thirty years ago when I was a young local preacher in the North of England. I had been invited to address the mid-week prayer meeting at a small Methodist chapel in a coal-mining village. The street was narrow, curving down from the main road on a sharp incline, and was dimly lit by gas lamps. It was late fall, and the evening was chilly and damp, a light mist enveloping the small stone building as the people gathered in the annex which served as a meeting place. Cold and unwelcoming at first, the room began to fill with the warmth of Christian fellowship as people came through the door and greeted one another—though no one spoke without first bowing for a moment of silent prayer. The opening hymn was followed by a prayer, a scripture reading, and then by more hymns, as the organist, who had to pump the instrument with his feet, found his second wind. After several choruses of favorite selections, he assumed his place among the rest of us, forehead glistening.

The leader of the meeting then took over, dominating the proceedings with a natural authority. He was a coal miner, standing tall and erect with the stiffness of those who spend their working hours bent double underground. He welcomed everyone by name, addressing each in turn with informal yet discerning remarks. All of his comments were received with openness by the persons concerned, including several rebukes. One had not been attending the mid-week meetings regularly: "We meet here *every* week, you know." Another had missed Sunday worship: "We'd all like to lie in of a morning, so *that's* no excuse." Yet another had been overheard using bad language at the coal mine: "People know you come here to chapel, and that makes a bad witness." And for those members of the choir who had apparently taken part in an argument before worship last Sunday evening: "Anyone could see what had been going on when you people came out to sing."

He also had words of praise and encouragement for those who had witnessed to their faith or who had been especially helpful in the community—words which in some instances were a surprise to the person concerned, and all of which drew sympathetic murmurs of appreciation from the rest of the gathering. One person had organized a fund-raising march for the mentally disabled. Another had been awarded a certificate of recognition for service to the local branch of the Red Cross. Another had been commended privately to the leader for his role at a recent meeting of the coal miners' trade union, and was now publicly commended by one who understood how courageously he had spoken. Each received a word of praise in turn. But the praise was not lavish. Clearly they had done no more than was expected of good Methodists. They had merely been faithful Christian disciples.

Throughout these remarks, the guidance and instruction of the leader were accepted unquestioningly, and his credentials have become clearer to me as the years have passed. Those who were rebuked gave the impression that they would have been disappointed had they not been called to task. Those who were praised and encouraged showed that they did not accept it as a personal congratulation, but rather as a token of their contribution to the witness of the chapel as a whole. It was, to coin a phrase, a good coaching session, and as I was given the lectern to deliver my message, I knew that the audience was as discerning as any I was ever likely to address. Spiritually, they were well attuned; and in terms of Christian obedience, they were seasoned. Moreover, they were hungry for one thing only—the authentic Word of the gospel to sustain them in their task, and to render their discipleship more effective. They were in the front line of the struggle for the coming reign of God, and they knew their need of support.

The key to all of this was the leader. It was clear that he belonged to their company, that he was one of them. He too worked in the coal mine; he too lived in the village; he too had children at the local school. But equally clearly he had accepted and had been granted a pivotal leadership role: not as a theologian, or as a Bible teacher, or as a preacher, but as a leader in discipleship, in the basics of Christian living in the world. In terms of the simple, straightforward guidelines that Jesus gave for discipleship, this man was one step ahead of the others. This did not make him an expert. But it gave the others an assurance that his guidance was trustworthy—and they accepted it, willingly.

This coal miner did not carry the title of class leader. As in many Methodist congregations, it had fallen into disuse. But his role in that meeting was an echo loud and clear of the office that once comprised the "sinews" of Methodism. If you have read this far, it is very possible that God is calling you to assume that role in the church of today; in which case, you should take the time to read further. And if the call grows stronger as you read, then you must answer it.

Chapter One

The Need for Leaders
in Discipleship

THE MYSTERY OF CHRISTIAN DISCIPLESHIP

Of all the mysteries that confront the Christian disciple—the mystery of sin, evil, and suffering, the mystery of death and resurrection, the mystery of God's love and redemption in Jesus Christ, the mystery of time and eternity, and the mystery of the coming reign of God—there is nothing more mysterious than Christian discipleship itself.

Let it quickly be said that the mystery does not lie in the call or the challenge of the Christian life. Those of us who have accepted the invitation to discipleship have been made aware of our conditions of service. We know that, as disciples of Jesus, we are called to affirm and embody his pronouncements that the day is coming when the first will be last and the last first, and when the meek, not the strong, will be in charge—pronouncements that will inevitably cause tensions with the world in which we live. We have willingly, if not always graciously, accepted the cost of walking with Jesus of Nazareth, because he was nothing if not candid about the life we could expect to lead:

> Do not think that I have come to bring peace to the earth; I have not come to bring peace, but a sword.
>
> > For I have come to set a man against his father,
> > and a daughter against her mother,
> > and a daughter-in-law against her mother-in-law;
> > and one's foes will be members of one's own household.
>
> Whoever loves father or mother more than me is not worthy of me; and whoever loves son or daughter more than me is not worthy of me; and whoever does not take up the cross and follow me is not worthy of me. Those who find their life will lose it, and those who lose their life for my sake will find it (Matt. 10:34-39).

1

There is nothing mysterious about these conditions, because we have known, or should have known about them from the outset. The mystery lies rather in why so many church members who profess the name of Jesus, who witness to his saving grace, and who take part regularly in so many aspects of congregational life and work, do not seem to take seriously what the scriptures have to say about the cost of discipleship. Jesus made clear that there were conditions to following him: that it would require commitment and self-denial; that it would mean accepting his lifestyle and following his teachings; and that it would mean taking seriously what he had to say about God's coming reign of love, peace and justice, on earth as in heaven.

LOOSE DISCIPLESHIP

It is hard to find a word that is used so widely in the church today yet defined so loosely as *disciple*. If Jesus meant what he said when he cautioned people not to follow him lightly, then his disciples should always count the cost very carefully beforehand (Luke 14:25-33). In this case the reality of congregational life in the United States of America would seem to indicate one of two things: either that the great majority of church members are not Christian disciples at all; or else that many millions of Christians in the North American church are in for a rude awakening when they finally discover what they agreed to be and to do when they answered the call to discipleship.

Not to mince words, Christian discipleship is presented by and large in our congregations today as an unqualified blessing. People are promised a heightened quality of life, a fulfillment of their gifts and graces, and participation in a supportive and loving community. Moreover, they are assured a spiritual relationship with a loving, parental God who is concerned for their personal welfare to a very marked degree. In short, they are offered a very good package of benefits indeed.

For those of us who view Christian discipleship somewhat differently—who do take seriously what Jesus told us to say and to do, who try to be faithful evangelists of the gospel of redemption and faithful stewards of God's creation, who seek to plumb the depths of the Word of God and teach others the ways of love and justice and peace, and who apply ourselves to the task of discipleship with the discipline that the word implies—for those of us who do endeavor to "take up the cross," this state of affairs is indeed mysterious.

MOMENTS OF RESENTMENT

Moreover, if the truth be told, there are times when the mystery exhausts our patience. We become resentful of what seems to be a constant compromise in our congregation's ministry and mission. We know that our own best efforts fall far short of costly discipleship; and in our less charitable moments, we find ourselves resenting fellow church members who appear to take their discipleship all too lightly. At best they seem to be indifferent or haphazard; at worst they seem to be self-centered and self-indulgent.

When we remember what Jesus said about becoming his disciple, and then place his words in the context of a typical congregation of today, we are chagrined by the contrast—not least because we ourselves are part of the problem. For when we invite people to come to church, we do not invite them to discipleship as Jesus defined the word. We do not ask them whether they are ready to leave their job, their home, their family, and their friends in order to follow Jesus Christ. When they become members, we do not press them to say whether they are ready to be ridiculed, humiliated, spurned, and persecuted for the sake of Jesus Christ. And we certainly do not ascertain whether they are ready to be tortured to death

Of course we don't. Questions such as these would frighten away new members before we could even interest them in a Sunday school class. Indeed, a list of such demands would probably reduce our existing membership rolls quite drastically. Yet the questions and the demands are scriptural (Matt. 5:11; Luke 6:22-23, 14:25-27), and there are those in every generation, including our own, who have paid just such a price to be a Christian disciple.[5] Moreover, there are faithful Christians throughout the world who witness and work for Christ in conditions that come far closer to the lifestyle he himself adopted during his earthly ministry—and the lifestyle he continues to adopt among the poor and disinherited of the earth. The unfinished work of Jesus Christ in the world challenges our congregational securities, and presses us to ask why we should provide so many churchly benefits for so many people who seem to contribute so little to the work of Jesus Christ.

MORE DISCIPLINE?

Does this mean, then, that we should insist on more costly membership requirements? Should we start reducing our rolls, cutting off those branches that do not bear good fruit? Would smaller but more disciplined congregations be better suited for the real work of Jesus Christ in the world? After all, Gideon did more with 300 seasoned warriors than with 30,000 volunteers. The early church was by no means a majority in the Roman empire. And early Methodism was far from being a mass movement in England: Its growth rate was less than fourteen a week during its first thirty years.[6] Yet in each instance, these small but deeply committed Christian disciples had an impact on the world out of all proportion to their numbers. There would seem to be a strong case for congregational pruning.

It is tempting to contemplate some such means of "quality control" in our churches today. From time to time, those of us who give so much of our resources and energy to our congregations become wistful about what it would be like to belong to a community of faith that was truly faithful, truly reliable, and truly committed to Jesus Christ. Yet when we face up to the reality of our own discipleship, we see only too clearly that we are very inadequate role models. By the same token, when we are realistic about our congregational ministry and mission, we know that the last thing we would ever do is exclude anyone from membership on grounds of inadequate faith. We are only too glad to see them come to church, whatever their commitment.

So we resign ourselves to the mystery. It seems that communities of faith, professedly dedicated to serving Jesus Christ, are fated to have a very mixed constituency—not least because those of us called upon to keep the church of Jesus Christ alive and healthy are far from consistent ourselves. And if it strikes us from time to time that we are carrying more than our fair share of congregational obligations, ranging from financial support and taking care of church buildings and grounds, to teaching in Sunday school and serving on the committees that seem to proliferate each year, we have no reason to complain. We should accept our duties and responsibilities with good grace, because even on our good days, we are merely fulfilling our minimal obligations. Besides, Jesus was very clear that we should leave all evaluations in God's hands (Matt. 7:1-55; Luke 6:37-42).

THE TWO-FOLD MINISTRY OF JESUS

There is, however, a more positive way of looking at these congregational contradictions. It does not resolve the mystery, but it helps those of us with churchly responsibilities to perform our duties with purpose rather than resignation. The insight lies in recognizing that there are two tracks to the ministry of Jesus—tracks we do not always take care to distinguish.

On the one hand, his ministry to people was unconditional. When five thousand were stranded in the desert without food, he fed them (Matt. 14:15-21). When he healed ten lepers, and only one of them came back to thank him, he did not make the other nine lepers diseased again to teach them good manners. He merely noted that the one who had returned to give thanks was a Samaritan (Luke 17:17). When his disciples wanted to send away those who had brought children to be blessed, Jesus laid his hands on them (Matt. 19:13-15). And when the people gathered around him, he told them parable after parable (Matt. 13:3; Mark 4:33). He did all of these things without any conditions at all—except that people should be open to receiving his gifts and willing to accept him for who he was. He had compassion on them, and he called them his flock, because they needed a shepherd to guide and enfold them (Matt. 9:36, 10:6; Mark. 6:34; John 10:1-6).

When it came to being his disciple, however, Jesus made people think very carefully about their decision. Indeed, he seemed to go out of his way to discourage them. For the discipleship to which Jesus invited his small, selected band of followers, was highly conditional. He stressed that it would mean leaving everything else behind in order to serve him. To love him would mean not only obeying his teachings, but following him all the way to the cross. As might be expected of someone with integrity, therefore, he advised people *not* to become his disciple unless they were willing to accept these conditions.

He told parables to make this altogether clear: the man who began to build a tower without calculating the cost, and became a subject of ridicule when he could not finish it (Luke 14:28-30); the king who realized that he could not fight against an opponent who outnumbered him two to one, and thus negotiated a peace before the confrontation (Luke 14:31-32). And we have the sobering word in John 6:66, that "many of his disciples turned back and no longer went about with him" because of his teachings.

FEED MY SHEEP

Jesus also impressed upon his disciples that they were not superior to other people. On the contrary, they were to make themselves everyone else's servant (Mk. 9: 33-5, 10:43-45). He made this
altogether clear when he himself washed their feet (John 13:1-17).
Specifically, the disciples of Jesus were to help him tend his flock.
When he fed the multitude in the desert, it was the disciples who
were called upon to distribute the bread and the fish (Matt.15:19;
Mark 6:41; Luke 9:16). And along with his commission to "make
disciples of all nations" (Matt. 28.19), he instructed Peter to feed his
sheep and his lambs—not once, but three times (John. 21:15-17).

Jesus did not use this imagery lightly. It was familiar to his
hearers, because they lived in a land where tending sheep was a
common livelihood. The first to be honored with the news of his
birth were shepherds, "keeping watch over their flock by night"
(Luke 2:8-20); and the nature and purpose of shepherding provided him with many rich parables for his teaching (Matt. 7:15,
12:11, 25:32; Luke 15:3-7; John 10:11-18).

A SHEPHERD'S SECRET

A personal experience may help to illustrate the point. My wife
and I spent the early years of our marriage living in the border
country between England and Scotland—the place where for centuries the border collie dog has been bred to run a hundred miles a
day herding flocks of sheep. The instinct of these dogs is uncanny.
They do, of course, receive signals from the shepherd—signals so
subtle that spectators are rarely aware of them. But the dogs also
act a great deal on their own initiative, knowing exactly when to
move toward a sheep, or to stand motionless, or to flank the flock
so that they will go where the shepherd wants them. At professional sheep trials, they are a thrill to watch.

We came to know one of these shepherds quite well, and one day
he told us a trade secret. "If you want to work a hundred sheep,"
he confided, "never try to work the whole flock at once. You'll have
chaos. There'll be sheep all over the place, and you'll be at your
wits' end. The way to work a hundred sheep is for you and the dog
first to get to know the six or seven leaders. Once you know the
leaders, and get them to do what you want, the rest will follow."

I have never forgotten this word of wisdom; and I have heard it from enough shepherds since then to know that it is a very open secret. On the assumption that animals have not changed all that much since the time of Jesus, it says a great deal about his use of sheep to illustrate his teachings. Most especially it sheds light on why some church members seem to take their discipleship more seriously than others: They are the leaders of the flock. They are more intentional about their discipleship because Jesus has identified them as leaders, and brought them more directly under his guidance—the guidance of the good shepherd. As they respond to the leadership of Christ, they in turn show the rest of the congregation the way ahead. The other members will follow willingly—if, that is, they know that the leaders are indeed following Jesus Christ. Just as important, they will follow if the leaders are welcomed as colleagues by the pastor and properly acknowledged in the life and work of the church.

TOO MUCH EXPERTISE

Unfortunately, in many of our congregations today this does not happen. These indigenous leaders of the flock are often mistrusted by the pastor and ignored by the congregation. It is rather assumed that Christian discipleship requires expert leadership, which only the pastor and professional staff can provide—a very mistaken assumption indeed. It is precisely what professional shepherds warn against: trying to work a flock without identifying the leaders already in place.

There are of course aspects of the Christian life in which skilled leadership is necessary, and where a little learning can be very mischievous. A good example of this is spiritual formation, which should not be undertaken without a great deal of training in the appropriate disciplines, especially when it involves therapeutic direction. Another example is interpreting the Bible, which likewise requires knowledgeable guidance. It is disturbing that so much Bible study still takes place with little more than the availability of the text and a self-appointed leader. Yet another example is that of social action, which usually requires much more than a concern for the disadvantaged if it is to be effective. There are places where well-meaning but ill-informed volunteers can do more harm than good in dealing with some of our contemporary social problems.

GETTING THE JOB DONE

On the other hand, there are some basic areas of discipleship where the pressing need is not expertise, or even competence, but merely getting the job done. And in these areas, the church is facing a leadership crisis of the first order. Ironically, there is no shortage of leadership in the more specialized areas of discipleship, where experts are readily available to help us with our particular gifts and graces. To use the same examples, spiritual direction has become a major emphasis in the church, with a wealth of outstanding authors and advisers; Bible study has a tremendous new energy in congregations right now, primarily because leading biblical scholars are making the scriptures come alive for ordinary people; while sociologists and anthropologists of religion are providing fascinating insights into our culture that give new clarity and focus to our social programs and strategies.

All of this expert leadership, however, begs a very important question. Who is actually *forming* Christian disciples in our congregations? Who is guiding them when they first set out on their journey with Christ? Who is helping them walk before the experts show them how to run? Who is showing them the ropes of *basic* Christian living in the world? It is a long time since these questions were asked in many congregations.

PRACTICING THE BASICS

The fact of the matter is that we have a dearth of leaders in basic discipleship. The implications of this for our congregational life are dealt with in Part One of the companion volume, *Forming Christian Disciples* (DR093B). They can be summarized, however, in a single observation: We have made Christian discipleship complicated primarily as an excuse to avoid obeying the teachings of Jesus Christ, which are really very simple.

One evidence of this, as we have noted, is the proliferation of experts in just about every dimension of the Christian life. Yet when we turn to the teachings of Jesus, to the *basics* of Christian discipleship, we find little if anything that requires expertise. When a rich man asked Jesus how he could inherit eternal life, there was nothing complicated about the reply: "Go, sell what you own, and give the money to the poor, and you will have treasure in heaven;

then come, follow me" (Mark 10:21). This did not require expertise, only resolve—which, as we know, he did not have. He was quite *able* to follow Jesus. But when faced with the reality, he was not *willing*.

At every turn of the page in the Gospels, we find simple and straightforward directives from Jesus. Feed the hungry, clothe the naked, visit the sick and the imprisoned (Matt. 25:31-46). Do not judge, do not condemn, and you will not be judged and condemned. Forgive, and you will be forgiven; give, and it will be given to you (Luke 6:37). A man was going down from Jerusalem to Jericho and fell into the hands of robbers. A Samaritan was moved with pity and took care of him. Go and do likewise (Luke 10:29-37). If you keep my commandments, you will abide in my love. This is my commandment, that you love one another as I have loved you (John 15:10,12).

DELAYING TACTICS

The problem with these simple teachings of Jesus has never been our inability to understand them, but our unwillingness to practice them. With all the ingenuity of teenagers seeking to avoid the family chores (and with the ready cooperation of our church experts), we have found every imaginable way of postponing our obedience to Jesus Christ—all the while, of course, claiming to be his disciples. The range of our church programs, the comfort of our church surroundings, and the time and energy we expend on our religious self-improvement, all are in marked contrast to the daily suffering of Christ's little ones across the face of our planet—the very ones Jesus commands us to serve. The loving rebuke of a Methodist leader from the Third World on a recent visit to the U.S.A. should make us wince: "You must be desperate to avoid loving your neighbors to have found so many ways of loving yourselves."

A rebuke such as this stings us because it is so patently deserved. If Christian discipleship means following Jesus of Nazareth, whose ministry was *to* the world, *in* the world, and *of* the world, and if we claim the identity of being his disciples, then we must expect to join him in that ministry of "good news to the poor, release to the captives, and recovery of sight to the blind" (Luke 4:18). We must also expect the world to treat us in the same way it treated him:

He was despised and rejected by others; a man of suffering and acquainted with infirmity . . . and we held him of no account (Isa. 53:3). He was in the world . . . yet the world did not know him. He came to what was his own, and his own people did not accept him (John 1:10-11).

With prospects such as these for our discipleship, it is little wonder that we seek delaying tactics. But the stories of costly servanthood from around the world continue to unsettle us. We know that those who claim to be disciples of Jesus Christ cannot evade their responsibilities indefinitely. We also know that in the North American church, we have delayed long enough.

FIRST STEPS

As with any major undertaking, the first steps in Christian discipleship are the most straightforward and also the most difficult. We read that when Jesus called Simon and Andrew, they immediately left their nets and followed him, as did James and John (Matt. 4:19-22). It sounds simple enough, but we should not overlook the significance of the step they took in becoming his disciples. Clearly they were convinced of his authority as a prophet and a teacher; but they were also prepared to trust his leadership. As Jesus himself put it, calling him "Lord, Lord" was not enough. They not only had to hear his words. They had to *act* on them (Luke 6:46).

This aspect of Christian discipleship has become very blurred in our thinking today, largely due to our delaying tactics. On the one hand, the greatest gift of the Christian life is faith in Jesus Christ. Precisely because it is a gift of the Holy Spirit, it requires just one thing of us: that we accept the forgiveness and reconciliation with God that Jesus has accomplished for us. The only condition of this gift is repentance, the decision to come back home and accept our place in God's family. The gift of faith is God's gracious initiative. We merely decide to accept it, or to reject it.

On the other hand, the gift of faith in Christ, important though it is, does not make us Christian disciples. It merely makes us *ready* to be Christ's disciples. To actualize our discipleship, to make it real, we must take our first steps, just like Simon, Andrew, James, and John. Discipleship requires more than a change of heart. It requires a change in our lives. It requires us not only to know Jesus Christ, but to walk with him. It requires us not only to hear his words, but to *act on them*.

MORE DELAYING TACTICS

It is at this point that our delaying tactics become little short of brilliant. Instead of taking our first steps with Christ, we stop to analyze our new relationship with him. Instead of acting on his words, we ponder them. Instead of accepting the gift of faith as an empowerment for our discipleship in the world, we seek deeper assurances of faith as a measure of our discipleship. In short, we use our faith as a way of putting off our discipleship—as a way of convincing ourselves about Jesus Christ rather than actually following him.

Yet the New Testament states quite the opposite. Our relationship with Christ does not depend on our inward assurance of faith, but on *doing* what he tells us to *do* (John 15:1-17). Thus, to claim we are disciples of Jesus Christ, but not to take the first steps in obedience to him, is a self-contradiction. In point of fact, it weakens our relationship with him. We do not need more faith in order to deepen our relationship with Jesus Christ. Rather, we need to obey Jesus Christ in order to deepen our faith—indeed, to sustain it. Our relationship with Christ deepens *as we obey*.

We shall have more to say about this preoccupation with faith (below, pp. 30-33). But there is something else that helps to explain our procrastinations: Protestants tend to be "wordy" people. Perhaps this is because printing was invented just before the Reformation; there are probably other reasons as well. But one thing is sure—we Protestants have consistently been fascinated by the written and spoken word in shaping our faith. And since one of the best ways to avoid doing something is to discuss it, we have often delayed the practice of our discipleship on the pretext of seeking to define it more clearly.

Had the first disciples adopted our delaying tactics, they would never have left their nets and their boats. Of course their faith in Jesus was not as strong as it later would become; and of course their understanding of his teachings was not as deep as it would become. The point is that they took their first steps *with whatever faith they had*. They actually followed Jesus, and in so doing they learned from him. Theirs was not a classroom education, but a schooling from someone whose words and actions were a constant example. They came to know him as they walked with him.

LEADING THE FLOCK

Walking with Jesus taught the disciples another important lesson. They had not been chosen merely to enjoy a special relationship with Jesus, but to be equipped for a special task. They did not see this at first. But eventually they understood that their relationship with Christ was for a purpose. They were to lead the family of God back home where they belonged—a family that was very much larger than they had imagined. For Jesus made clear to them that the family of God extended far beyond the chosen people of Israel (Matt. 15:21-28; John 10:16). Indeed, it was love for the whole world that had impelled God to take human form (John 3:16).

This continues to be the task of those who are called to Christian discipleship today. The flock of Jesus Christ, far larger than any of us can imagine, still needs to be brought home. Many stubbornly resist the invitation, and some are far into the wilderness. Yet instinctively they know that they need to come home, and Christian disciples must show them the way. The flock is hungry for the bread of life and thirsty for the living water, and the church must be as generous with these gracious gifts as was Jesus himself. Our doors must be wide open, and our supply must be limitless.

This means, of course, that we must also be ready for people to respond to our invitation, and come through our open doors. As we reach out to the flock of Jesus in the world, people are going to accept God's gracious gift of faith in Christ. They are going to come back home. Moreover, as they come to church week by week and are fed by the ministries of word and sacrament, the grace they receive will not be inactive in their lives. The Holy Spirit will bring them to the point where they too will want to become Christian disciples. They too will want to take their first steps in following Jesus Christ, and they will ask us to show them the way.

GUIDANCE IN THE FIRST STEPS

The church so often fails these prospective Christian disciples. It is not a question of providing them with expert advice and instruction. That will come later. At this starting point in their discipleship they need only to be shown the basics—the first steps in following Christ. And for this, they merely need the guidance of comrades who can show them the way. Yet this is the very leadership seldom to be found in the church today. What is worse, seldom is the need for it even acknowledged.

The church has no excuse for neglecting such a foundational dimension of its life and work. For one thing, this sort of leadership is commonplace in other walks of life. When we join a new organization, or start a new job, there is always someone to "show us the ropes" or give us a "hands-on" demonstration. Older students at school are asked to help younger students; members of sports teams coach new players in the essentials of the game; military or drill squad leaders train new recruits; section leaders take players through their scales in an orchestra or band; the examples are endless. In each instance, the newcomers willingly accept basic guidance and supervision from those who "know the ropes."

Yet when new members are welcomed into a congregation, and especially people who are just starting out in the Christian life, rarely is there someone to "show them the ropes" of discipleship. If anyone is assigned to help them at all, it is usually to make them "feel at home," or to "assimilate" them into church activities; and this is not at all the same thing. A great deal of energy is likely to be expended getting them involved in program and administration. New members will find themselves recruited very quickly for any number of task force or committee responsibilities. But in terms of basic Christian living in the world, very rarely do they find down-to-earth guidance and collegiality.

By the same token, when church membership classes are held as a condition of joining a congregation, all too often they tend to focus on basic introductory doctrines rather than challenging and encouraging new members to discover the true meaning of these teachings through Christian living in the world. This can easily leave them preoccupied with refining their beliefs instead of putting them into practice—a habit that is very hard to break once the world begins to test and try their faith, and their pilgrimage with Jesus Christ begins in earnest.

LEADERSHIP CREDENTIALS

Rather than pastoral care or doctrinal instruction, disciples setting out in the Christian life need a helping hand from someone who knows the way ahead just a little better than they do—someone who can show them by example. This is by far the best credential for leading in discipleship. It combines practical experience with shared pilgrimage, making the leader at once a guide and a fellow traveler. The training for such a role is almost always acquired "on the job," and the respect accorded by those who follow is usually well earned. But since our delaying tactics have made discipleship such a complicated and sensitive issue (see above, p. 8), it is a leadership role that has come to rest almost entirely today with the pastor and the church professional staff.

The problem is that pastors and church staff rarely have the credentials for this basic leadership in discipleship. For one thing, they are trained in very particular areas of the Christian life, undergoing rigorous intellectual and spiritual preparation for their various ministries. It is not a good use of pastoral resources to expend these skills on basic guidance in the Christian life—to say nothing of the routine administration of the church.

Just as important is the fact that professional church staff seldom practice their discipleship in the same worldly arena as the members of their congregations. They are almost always at a distance from where ordinary Christians live and work and witness. Just as the authority of the coal miner at the midweek prayer meeting came from living out his discipleship alongside the other members (see above, p. xxii), so leaders in discipleship today need to be in the front line alongside the disciples they endeavor to lead, witnessing for Christ at times and in places where pastors and church staff are unlikely to be present. The most important credential for these leaders is to walk with Christ in the world *alongside* the people they are leading.

A LEADERSHIP QUESTION

If these are valid leadership credentials, they raise a very important question. Assuming that these basic leaders in discipleship are simply "showing people the ropes" as fellow pilgrims, is there anything that distinguishes them from other church members? It may well be important to stress their peer relationship with the congregation and their companionship with those they are leading. But if there is no real distinction between them and other church members, why recognize them as leaders at all? Why give them authority or even permission to guide the discipleship of others?

There is indeed a distinction between these leaders in basic discipleship and the remainder of the congregation; but it is a distinction that in no way implies a separation. Just as Jesus called some to be his disciples, yet made clear that his flock was one (John

10:16), and just as Paul identified differing gifts within the church, yet made clear that the Body was one under the headship of Christ (Eph. 4:11,15-16), so the distinctive role of leader in discipleship does not imply separation from the rest of the congregation. Yet they are different nonetheless: they have taken a further step in their walk with Christ.

A TOUCHY QUESTION

The question—and it is a very touchy one—is how to draw this distinction without removing the inseparability, the comradeship, and the peer relationship with other church members, all of which are critical aspects of their leadership. Even more important, how do we draw the distinction without appearing to create a clique in the congregation? For if there is an issue guaranteed to raise the temperature of any discussion about leadership in the church today, it is elitism.

To some extent, of course, the recognition of any such leadership role is bound to be controversial in our present climate of personalized discipleship. It is so long since church members were presented with any clearcut guidelines for following Jesus Christ in the world that the very notion of someone being more advanced or experienced in their discipleship is sure to raise objections. It is widely assumed in contemporary church life that everyone who is a Christian disciple is walking with Christ, albeit along different paths. Thus the idea that they might be following Christ more or less faithfully, and that good leadership might improve their discipleship, will not sit easily with those who are accustomed to asking for guidance exclusively from Christ himself.

AMATEURS AND PROFESSIONALS

While there is no way to avoid such questions, it might be helpful to draw an analogy. There are many areas of life in which we make a distinction between amateurs and professionals. The distinction is certainly not in terms of skill, for an outstanding amateur is better than a mediocre professional any day. Nor is it a matter of payment for services. Again, creative ways are always found to reimburse good amateurs far more lucratively than run-of-the-mill professionals.

The difference between an amateur and a professional lies in the meaning of the two words. The word *amateur* come from the Latin *amator*, meaning "one who loves." Amateurs do something because they like to do it. Professionals, on the other hand, "profess" their profession. They declare it as the activity, the skill, the craft, the career, by which they wish everyone else to recognize them and know them. It is foundational to their very identity.

In a word, the difference between the professional and the amateur is *accountability*. On a good day, amateurs can enjoy success, and accept all due praise and accolades. But on a bad day they always have an excuse: "Don't judge me by this—I'm only an amateur." On a given day, amateurs may feel good and perform with gusto; on another day they may feel like opting out, and do so without disgrace. Professionals, on the other hand, declare precisely the opposite: "I *want* you to judge me by my work. I insist on it. Never mind how I am feeling on any particular day—you can count on me to fulfill my obligations."

It is this sort of declaration that distinguishes leaders in discipleship from the rest of the congregation. These are the members who have reached a stage in their walk with Christ where they are willing to be evaluated. They are ready to check and be checked in their obedience to Christ's teachings. They realize that this "professionalism" cannot be exercised without collegiality: that they need the support, the advice, and the correction of others who have reached a similar point in their pilgrimage, and who share with them the desire to be more trustworthy and reliable servants of Jesus Christ. In short, they are willing to be assessed as a Christian—indeed, as a person—by their discipleship.

This "professional" commitment does not necessarily mean greater accomplishment in Christian discipleship. It does not make these people experts in church life and work. It does not give them higher intellect or a more winsome personality. And it certainly does not elevate them to sainthood. The difference lies in their application to the task in hand. Their discipleship is no longer haphazard, no longer subject to whim or mood. Following the teachings of Christ is now a matter of accountability, of honoring their obligations. They make their obedience to Jesus Christ foundational to their very identity. Those whom they endeavor to lead in discipleship may well outshine them in the finer points of the Christian life, but never in their commitment to the basics. They are the very stuff of congregational leadership, and we badly need them today.

A MODEL FROM EARLY METHODISM

All of this brings us to the office of class leader. Of the many models for basic Christian leadership in the history of the church, there is none more suited to the needs of our congregations. Not only were class leaders the key to the organization of John Wesley's early Methodist societies; they also formed and fostered the discipleship of this eighteenth century movement that was to give birth to a major new Protestant denomination.

The fact that John Wesley entrusted them with so much responsibility; the fact that they were peers of the class members they were appointed to lead; the fact that the weekly meetings they held with their classes were regarded by Wesley as the "sinews" of the Methodist movement; and the fact that they have left us with a wealth of practical Christian wisdom; all of this, and much more, make it imperative that we find out who these men and women were, and what they did—and if at all possible, recover the tradition of their leadership.

FOR REFLECTION

1. How often are you confronted by the mysteries listed in the opening paragraph of this chapter?

2. Do you find discipleship loosely defined in your congregation? (p. 2)

3. Do we need more "quality control" in our congregations to-day? (p. 4)

4. What do you make of the suggestion that there were two tracks to Jesus' ministry? (p. 5)

5. Does the rebuke from the Third World Methodist leader make you wince? (p. 9) Why, or why not?

6. Do you find yourself trying to obey Jesus with whatever faith you have? Or do you seek more faith in order to obey him? (p. 11)

7. Can you recall who "showed you the ropes" of Christian discipleship? (p. 13)

8. Did your membership training in the church consist of "right belief," or "right action," or both? (p. 13)

9. Do you agree that leaders in discipleship are those who have "taken a further step in their walk with Christ?" (p. 15)

10. Do you find the distinction between "amateur" and "professional" helpful? (pp. 15-16) Why, or why not?

Chapter Two

The Origin of Class Leaders

THE EARLY METHODIST MOVEMENT

Before we explore the origin of class leaders, it will be important to understand something about the nature and purpose of the early Methodist movement. The companion volume, *Covenant Discipleship* (DR091B), describes this historical background in more detail, so we need only be reminded here of the salient points. First, we must remember that Methodism did not begin as an independent church, and that its chief founder and leader, John Wesley, did not intend it to become a church. He made clear at the outset that he was fostering "societies" of men and women who, "having the form and seeking the power of Godliness, united in order to pray together, to receive the word of exhortation, and to watch over one another in love, that they may help each other to work out their salvation."[7]

Wesley saw these societies as a source of spiritual renewal *within* the church, and constantly resisted any tendency to separate into new congregations. His vision was ultimately thwarted, in part by the negative attitude of the Church of England, and in part by the course of history, which led to the forming of the Methodist Episcopal Church in North America. Even so, he remained loyal to the Church of England to the end of his life, and urged the Methodists in England to do likewise.[8]

In the words of Rupert Davies, it was Wesley's profound conviction, shared with his brother Charles, that "the church of Christ is one church, that the Church of England is its embodiment in England, and that to divide the Church of England would be a sin of terrible magnitude, unless it had committed the prior sin of commanding things contrary to the Word of God—which the Church of England had not done."[9] Quite apart from the scriptural and doctrinal reasons against separation, Wesley was well aware of the practical dangers. If a movement such as Methodism began to plot a course to separate from the church, it would be diverted

19

from its original purpose. The immediate wants and needs of the society members, to say nothing of their dissatisfaction with the Church of England, would begin to take precedence over the more lasting and significant mission of the church—a mission that had already spanned seventeen centuries and was still not fulfilled.

AFFECTION FOR THE CHURCH

Thus it was Wesley's constant concern that the Methodist societies should remain within the Church of England. He repeatedly urged this, not only as a point of discipline, but also as a matter of loyalty, and he made very clear where his own affections lay:

> If we continue in the Church, not by chance, or for want of thought, but upon solid and well-weighed reasons, then we should never speak contemptuously of the Church, or anything pertaining to it. In some sense it is the mother of all who have been brought up therein. We ought never to make her blemishes a matter of diversion, but rather of solemn sorrow before God. We ought never to talk ludicrously of them; no, not at all, without clear necessity. Rather we should conceal them, as far as ever we can without bringing guilt upon our own conscience. And we should all use every rational and scriptural means to bring others to the same temper and behaviour. I say, all; for if some of us are thus minded, and others of an opposite spirit and behaviour, this will breed a real schism among ourselves. It will of course divide us into two parties, each of which will be liable to perpetual jealousies, suspicion, and animosities against the other. Therefore on this account likewise it is expedient to the highest degree that we should be tender of the Church to which we belong.[10]

TRUE FREEDOM OF DISCIPLESHIP

As Wesley saw it, only by staying within the church could Methodists have true freedom of discipleship. As long as they regarded themselves as part of a larger Christian family, they were free to be disciplined servants of Christ. The fact that they were committed to a more accountable form of discipleship—a "methodical" discipleship—did not thereby denigrate other church members, tenuous though the discipleship of many eighteenth century parishioners might have been. Problems would arise, however, if those who adopted this accountable discipleship of the societies were to regard themselves as superior followers of Christ, thereby relegating everyone else to an inferior status. The freedom of discipleship would then be lost in the bondage of spiritual pride and elitism.

Wesley was determined to prevent this error from infecting his societies. Those who did not become Methodists could still belong to the larger church. They were still part of the family of God. He made clear to his members that they were not to think of themselves as having any kind of monopoly on God's grace:

> The thing which I was greatly afraid of all this time, and which I resolved to use every possible method of preventing, was narrowness of spirit, a party zeal, a being straitened in our own bowels; that miserable bigotry which makes so many unready to believe that there is any work of God but among themselves. I thought it might be a help against this frequently to read, to all who were willing to hear, the accounts I received from time to time of the work which God is carrying on in the earth, both in our own and other countries, not among us alone, but among those of various opinions and denominations. For this I allotted one evening in every month. And I find no cause to repent my labour. It is generally a time of strong consolation to those who love God, and all mankind for his sake; as well as of breaking down the partition walls which either the craft of the devil or the folly of men has built up; and of encouraging every child of God to say (O when shall it once be?), 'Whosoever doth the will of my Father which is in heaven, the same is my brother and sister and mother.'[11]

PRIVILEGED SERVANTHOOD

This breadth of outlook is no less essential in our own day and age. If we are to have leaders in discipleship, persons who lead by example, there must be a clear assurance that others are not thereby disadvantaged. As we noted in Chapter One, this simple truth is pivotal to any concept of leadership in the Christian life, and the point is worth emphasizing.

There are two issues involved. On the one hand, it is important for Christian disciples to understand that their relationship with

Christ does not bring them privileged status in the family of God. Jesus was at pains to explain this to his disciples, and it was the occasion of the first major confrontation in the early church, when Paul had to make clear to Peter that the gospel was for Gentiles no less than for Jews (Gal. 2:11-21).

The second issue is perhaps even more important for the church of today. If we hear the call to a discipleship that is more accountable, or more costly, does this mean that others are in disfavor with God for not doing likewise? This is a question that leaves many potential leaders in discipleship diffident about accepting such a call, because of genuine concern about their fellow church members, to say nothing of their family and friends.

We must therefore be very clear that such an inference is not at all scriptural. Suppose the call of Jesus to his first disciples had required them not only to leave their homes and their work, but also to accept that the loved ones they were leaving behind were in disfavor with God for not joining them. The very thought is offensive. Quite apart from the spiritual issues involved—and they are considerable—good manners and good taste dictate that, whatever the nature of our own call to discipleship, others are not disparaged by our response. On the contrary, the call to accountable discipleship is a call to service. Our costly commitment is not for our own benefit, but for the sake of Christ—and everyone in Christ's family. Our sole privilege is that of servanthood.[12]

SPIRIT AND STRUCTURE IN THE CHURCH

For all these reasons, Wesley spent considerable time and effort in trying to keep the Methodist societies within the Church of England. The principle he followed was that of *ecclesiolae in ecclesia* (little churches in the big church). The phrase was particularly associated with German Pietism, and referred to small house groups, *collegia pietatis*, convened in the late seventeenth century by a Lutheran pastor, Phillip Jakob Spener, in order to pursue a more intentional form of discipleship.[13] The concept came to have an even wider connotation in the various Protestant revivals and reform movements that subsequently appeared throughout Europe, and to this day it states a very important truth about the ministry and mission of the church as a whole.

Ecclesiolae in ecclesia reminds us that on the one hand the church is a spiritual community. It consists of persons who have been brought together by the Holy Spirit to be formed into the Body of Christ. Accordingly there must be freedom in the church to function with all the diversity of spiritual gifts and graces in a Body of which Christ is the head (Rom. 12; 1 Cor. 12). Without this spiritual freedom, the church will become self-serving, just like every other human institution, and will formalize the gospel into merely human traditions.

On the other hand, the church is a community of human beings. It consists of people who live in the world and are part of human society. Along with spiritual freedom, therefore, there must be disciplinary structure. Without agreement on doctrine and practice, and without some regulation as to ministry and mission, even a community devoted to Jesus Christ will end up with impossibly diffuse aims and purposes. Instead of spiritual freedom, there will be spiritualized anarchy.

When Christians truly seek to obey Jesus Christ, they take both of these churchly dimensions seriously, and hold them in a creative tension: *ecclesiolae IN ecclesia*. The spiritual freedom of the little church prevents discipleship from becoming unduly regulated or legalistic; the doctrine and structure of the large church guard against spiritual license and excess. When equal emphasis is given to spirit and structure, the ministry and mission of the church are powerful and healthy. But when this balance is not maintained, and undue weight is given to either its spiritual or its structural life, the work of Jesus Christ in the world is seriously handicapped. An unduly spiritualized church withdraws from the world that Jesus came to save. An unduly structured church becomes insensitive to the promptings of the Holy Spirit.

SPIRITUAL RENEWAL

The history of Christianity shows that when the church becomes insensitive in this way, and allows itself to be captivated by its own institutional life, the Holy Spirit does not give up, but moves in its midst with particular power. We see this in the rich diversity of religious orders in the Roman Catholic Church; and in Protestantism, we see it in the various forms of *ecclesiolae in ecclesia*. Indeed, when John Wesley assumed leadership of the early Methodist movement, he did not have to invent a pattern of church reform. There was one in place with which he was already very familiar, and in which he had to some degree taken part.

Toward the end of the seventeenth century, a number of "religious societies" had appeared in the Church of England. These consisted of young men (the inclusion of women in Methodist societies was a mark of Wesley's leadership) who wished to apply themselves more intentionally to devotional disciplines and practical good works among the poor. They had direct links with German Pietism, and they developed a coordinated network that was still in place during Wesley's formative years. By the time Wesley began his itinerant ministry in the late 1730s they had lost their initial momentum. But they provided a foundation for much of early Methodism, and many of them gave practical support to Wesley when he most needed it.[14]

OBEDIENT DISCIPLESHIP

In addition to many of the features of the religious societies, Wesley adopted one of their most important principles: Methodists were not to concern themselves with the doctrines and polity of the established Church of England. These were in place, and did not require further amendment. One of Wesley's earliest publications was *The Doctrine of Salvation, Faith, and Good Works* (1738), drawn from the sixteenth century *Homilies* of the Church of England; and he regarded the Anglican *Book of Common Prayer* as a solid and scriptural basis for all liturgical practice.

The focus of the Methodist societies was rather to be that of an obedient discipleship, consisting on the one hand of the practice of the basic disciplines of the Christian life, clearly laid out in the scriptures and tradition of the church, but largely ignored by the great majority of the church. On the other hand, it emphasized the spiritual freedom of an authentic walk with Christ, in which the promptings of the Holy Spirit take the disciple well beyond minimal observance of God's law.

Wesley viewed both of these dimensions as indispensable to faithful discipleship. The Christian life does not consist solely of rules and regulations. There must be a relationship with the risen Christ and a responsiveness to the Holy Spirit. But by the same token, a spiritual relationship with Christ that does not demonstrate obedience to his teachings is irresponsible and ultimately self-indulgent. The righteousness of the obedient disciple must exceed, not dispense with, the righteousness of the Scribes and Pharisees (Matt. 5:20).

RELIGIOUS COMMON SENSE

More than anything else, it is this understanding of discipleship that explains the early Methodist movement. The great privilege and freedom of the Christian life is the relationship of the individual believer with the risen Christ. The "inner witness" of the Holy Spirit provides an assurance that brings each disciple into an intimacy with God, a communion that truly passes all understanding. In this very intimacy, however, lies the subtle danger of spiritual self-deception. Christ may be reliable in this relationship, but we are not. For one thing, we are still affected by our sinful condition, even though we are forgiven and reconciled with God: we still harbor residual resistance against the Holy Spirit. For another thing, we live in a world that is strongly resistant to God's grace, and we find ourselves persistently affected by its waywardness.

Wesley understood this only too well as he endeavored to shape and guide the discipleship of the men and women who looked to him for direction. The early Methodists understood it too; and while they rejoiced in their spiritual relationship with Christ, they also exercised common sense. They knew that living in a sinful world rendered their spiritual insights suspect unless they had some means, some method, of plotting a course of faithful discipleship.

PASTORAL OVERSIGHT

The story of how the best method for this was discovered—class leaders and class meetings—is a striking example of the grace of God at work in the ordinary things of life. After the Wesley brothers and their colleagues had been preaching in the open air for several years, it became clear that some form of pastoral oversight would be required for the Methodist societies. Those who joined were often in need of basic orientation in the doctrines and disciplines of the church. And even when people were familiar with the church, they often lacked the more disciplined Christian lifestyle that was expected of Methodists.

According to Wesley's own account, they stumbled on the idea of class meetings and class leaders. In February, 1742, the Bristol society was discussing how to clear its building debt, and the solution they adopted was to divide the membership into sub-groupings of twelve, called *classes*, each with a *leader* who would collect the weekly contributions. It was soon found that the regular contact between the leaders and their respective class members also provided pastoral opportunities. As Wesley put it, having class leaders was an excellent way of "coming to a sure and thorough knowledge of each person."[15] The leaders were those members of the societies who could "not only receive the contributions, but also watch over the souls of their brethren."[16]

MUTUAL ACCOUNTABILITY

Thus it was that the grace of God brought about one of the simplest yet most effective methods for pastoral oversight the church has ever known. Within a year, the *classes* had become *class meetings*, in part to make the collection of monies by the leaders more convenient, but also to allow the concerns of each member to be shared by the class as a whole. This in turn gave rise to a dynamic of mutual accountability, which in and of itself came to be a significant means of pastoral support and oversight. Indeed, "watching over one another in love" was not only an effective pastoral method. It was also a powerful means of grace. In their weekly meetings the members shared their experiences. They prayed together. They affirmed and, if need be, corrected each other. Perhaps most important of all, as their open obedience to Christ and his teachings increasingly brought them social and religious isolation, the class meeting gave them a strong sense of identity as Christ's disciples in the world.

Nor were the class meetings the only form of small group within the early Methodist societies. There were *bands*, which in fact predated the classes by several years. These were more intimate groupings, in which there was a true spirit of mutual confession, not least because they were restricted to members who had experienced "justifying faith" and could testify to the "new birth" in their spiritual lives. There were also *select societies*, consisting of those members who were "going on to perfection"—who were sufficiently advanced in the spiritual life to be ready for the deepest and most searching form of spiritual consultation.

Yet it was the class meeting that became the basic sub-division of the Methodist societies, the place where members first learned to "watch over one another in love," and the place where weekly attendance was non-negotiable. Failure to attend regularly meant a period of probation followed by termination of membership if the problem was not rectified. Attendance was regulated by the issue of a quarterly class ticket, obtainable only after an examination by the preacher, and without which one was not in good standing. And while fellowship and mutual support were important components of these weekly meetings, the central element was an accountability for faithful discipleship. This much is clear from Wesley's publication of the *General Rules* for the societies in February, 1743, just one year after the meeting in Bristol at which the first class leaders had been appointed.[17]

THE NEED FOR MUTUAL SUPPORT

The clergy of the eighteenth century Church of England were for the most part indifferent or even hostile toward such pastoral oversight. Many of them did not understand the nature of the "new birth" which was at the cutting edge of Wesley's preaching, nor did they regard common people as having the capacity for spiritual development. Yet the people who responded to Wesley's message demonstrated that they were not at all common in their capacity for disciplined Christian living. Not only did they have deep spiritual discernment, but they also took seriously their Christian obligations. The nickname of "Methodist" stayed with them primarily because they were methodical in their efforts to obey the teachings of Jesus. And in eighteenth century England, this was more than enough to distinguish them from the average churchgoer.

As with any lifestyle different from that of society at large, this made the early Methodists marked people, which in turn meant that they needed one another for support as well as accountability. To witness to Jesus Christ in the world and to follow his teachings required the *koinonia* of Christian community no less than the *kerygma* of the gospel; and it was this that gave the class meeting such a ready acceptance among the Methodist societies. Wesley's own words put it well:

> It can scarce be conceived what advantages have been reaped from this little prudential regulation. Many now happily experienced that Christian fellowship of which they had not so much as an idea before. They began to 'bear one another's burdens', and 'naturally to care for each other'. As they had daily a more intimate acquaintance with, so they had a more endeared affection for each other. And 'speaking the truth in love,' they grew · up into him in all things which is the head, even Christ.[18]

THE CLASS LEADER

The key to all of this was the class leader. Important though it was for the members to watch over one another in love, the class leaders were the ones who made it possible to do this. To the extent that they were responsible for convening the classes, for directing the weekly meetings, and for guiding the members in their walk with Christ, they fulfilled a pastoral role that Wesley himself could not possibly have provided. Moreover, these men and women were the most direct link in a line of authority that extended from Wesley to the membership of the societies as a whole—a line of authority that kept English Methodism connected to the Church of England throughout Wesley's lifetime, and also provided legitimacy for the new Methodist Episcopal Church in the United States of America.

They did not, however, acquire their pastoral authority quickly or easily. When the office was initially introduced, there were objections that the leaders were "insufficient for the work," and had "neither gifts nor grace for such an employment." [19] Then, as now, people chafed under leadership that they did not at first regard as necessary. But Wesley stood his ground, and in due course the class leaders acquired the respect and the loyalty of their members. There were exceptions, of course, and Wesley was quick to remove unsuitable leaders when their lack of gifts and graces was brought to his attention. [20] But their pivotal role in nurturing the discipleship of the societies established them, in the words of a contemporary observer, as "the body politic" of Methodism. [21] They were as spiritual a group of leaders as the church has ever produced.

DISCIPLINARY OVERSIGHT

In addition to pastoral oversight, the class leaders also fulfilled a disciplinary function in the societies. As stated in the *General Rules*, their business was:

1. To see each person in his class, once a week at the least, in order to inquire how their souls prosper;
   To advise, reprove, comfort, or exhort, as occasion may require.
   To receive what they are willing to give toward the relief of the poor.
2. To meet the Minister and the stewards of the Society once a week in order:

> To inform the minister of any that are sick, or of any that are disorderly and will not be reproved.
> To pay in to the stewards what they have received of their several classes in the week preceding.[22]

While these duties were always subordinate to the authority of the preacher, in practice they gave the class leader a great deal of disciplinary power. He or she (from an early date, Wesley appointed women as well as men to the office) was the first person with whom a prospective member of a society discussed the conditions of membership. There was a probationary period of three months, during which a note would be issued for admission to society gatherings as well as the weekly class meetings. At the end of this time, the opinion of the leader would be sought in deciding whether or not to admit the new member.

The leaders also kept attendance records of the class meetings, on which they evaluated the spiritual maturity of each class member, and ensured that the *General Rules* were observed by everyone under their care. Because they were entrusted with so much disciplinary authority, once every three months they themselves were examined by Wesley or one of his preachers to ensure that they were fulfilling their obligations no less than their members. These examinations were also the occasion of issuing quarterly *class tickets* to members in good standing, a disciplinary measure which proved to be a "quiet and inoffensive method of removing any disorderly member."[23]

RESISTANCE TO DISCIPLINE

Needless to say, there were objections to these examinations, not least because Wesley declared their purpose to be the separation of "the precious from the vile."[24] The idea of evaluating behavior as a means of forming Christian disciples raised as many questions then as it does today, especially for those who regard discipleship as a highly personal matter, definable solely in terms of personal faith. This is well illustrated by an account in Wesley's *Journal* of a quarterly examination which he himself held at the town of Gateshead in 1747:

> On Monday, Tuesday, and Thursday I examined the classes. I had been often told it was impossible for me to distinguish the precious from the vile, without the miraculous discernment of

spirits. But I now saw, more clearly than ever, that this might be done, and without much difficulty, supposing only two things: first, courage and steadiness in the examiner; secondly, common sense and common honesty in the leader of each class. I visit, for instance, the class in the Close of which Robert Peacock is the leader. I ask, "Does this and this person in your class live in drunkenness or any outward sin? Does he go to church, and use the other means of grace? Does he meet you as often as he has opportunity?" Now, if Robert Peacock has common sense, he can answer these questions truly; and if he has common honesty, he will. And if not, some other in his class has both, and can and will answer for him. Where is the difficulty, then, of finding out if there be any disorderly walker in this class, and, consequently, in any other? *The question is not concerning the heart, but the life.* And the general tenor of this I do not say cannot be known, but *cannot be hid* without a miracle.[25]

MATTERS OF HEART AND LIFE

There could be no clearer statement of the nature and purpose of class leaders and of the Methodist movement as a whole. Yet it is on this very issue that Wesley is so often misunderstood. Throughout his writings, he is quite explicit that forgiveness and reconciliation with God are matters of the heart: justification is by grace, with the sole condition of faith. But discipleship, as his account of the Gateshead examination makes clear, is essentially a matter of life— of how one *lives.*

Of course it is God alone who ultimately knows what is in a person's heart. But when this spiritual truth is made the sole criterion of Christian living in the world, it opens the door to self-deception, and can quickly become an excuse to avoid the basic obligations of discipleship. However spiritually attuned and well intentioned Christian disciples might be, discerning the will of God through personal, inward communion is only part of the walk with Christ. Much of the time there is the routine (and often the drudgery) of meeting the needs of fellow human beings—tasks we would rather avoid. As Wesley astutely observes, how a person lives will always be a good indication of what is in a person's heart. Finding that out does not require extraordinary spiritual perception. If anyone needs a miracle, it is the person who tries to hide what is in the heart, from God or from anyone else.

SPIRITUALIZED DISCIPLESHIP

This issue more than any other impedes the development of leaders in discipleship for today's church. The way to strengthen faith in Christ is to do what Christ commands: to follow his basic, down-to-earth, practical teachings. Yet disciplinary directives seem to cause as much offense today as they did in Wesley's time. The objections stem from a deeply held conviction that forgiveness and reconciliation with God through Christ are the essence of Christian discipleship; and since there can be no human evaluation of such a deeply spiritual encounter, Christ alone can judge a person's discipleship. A leader in discipleship, therefore, should merely help people to sustain the faith on which their discipleship depends. What they do with that faith is the concern of no one but themselves and Christ.

This spiritualized discipleship is precisely what Wesley was at pains to counter in the early Methodist movement. He saw the importance of a vital faith relationship with God through Christ; but he also saw the danger of leaving this relationship unstructured and undisciplined. As a result, he preached both faith *and* works, and was persistently attacked for so doing: by Anglicans who regarded his affirmation of the new birth and personal faith as fanatical; and by evangelicals who regarded his rules for Christian living as legalistic and works-righteous. Yet his insights into these truths remain pivotal to a clear understanding of transformational leadership, which in turn is the key to faithful discipleship and congregational vitality in the church.

DISCIPLINED RELATIONSHIPS

The key lies in what at first seems to be a paradox: Faithful discipleship is relational *because* it is disciplined, and disciplined *because* it is relational. This strikes us as inconsistent, conditioned as we are by faith-centered discipleship and self-preoccupied congregations, not to mention the individualism and consumerism of our culture.[26] Under these influences, we tend to view relationships—and most especially our relationship with Christ—as a series of mutual impulses which can and should transcend the routine and the commonplace things of life. When the impulses are strong, our good works are a spontaneous overflow of goodwill, and our obedience to Christ seems to be the most natural thing in the world. But when the impulses weaken, as frequently they do, all too often we assume it is the relationship that has gone wrong; whereas the problem is the more obvious (and more easily corrected) inconsistency of our obedience to Jesus Christ.

Wesley warned his society members against this in the *General Rules*, where he urged Methodists to "trample under foot that enthusiastic doctrine of devils, that 'we are not to do good unless our heart be free to it.'"[27] The relationship with Christ established by the new birth has much spiritual spontaneity, yet this alone will not sustain it. Faith in Christ has to be tested, tempered, seasoned, and refined, through obedience to his teachings. Discipleship means following Christ's commands, not only by spiritual impulse, but also by routine, commonplace, methodical living in the world, for which he has given us some clear, down-to-earth guidelines. Over and again we find Jesus directing us to acts of neighborly compassion and justice, without which our acts of worship and devotion have a distinctly hollow ring (Matt. 5:23-24; Lk. 12:1-3).

COMPANIONSHIP WITH CHRIST

When we truly seek to follow Christ, in deed as well as in word, by action as well as by intent, we come to know the supreme privilege of Christian discipleship: companionship with Christ along the way. Instead of looking for Christ in the extraordinary experiences of life, we find him in the routine and the commonplace. When we apply ourselves to acts of compassion and justice, we find our worship and devotion filled with deeper spiritual communion.

The reason is very simple: This is the nature of the Christ with whom we are walking—if, that is, we really *want* to walk with him.[28] For walking with Christ is very different from merely receiving his blessings. It means getting to know him in depth: his concerns, his passions, his anger with the pain and suffering of little children, and his sense of urgency for the unfinished task of preparing this world for the coming reign of God. In other words, the longer we walk with Christ, the more demanding it becomes. It requires a discipleship, not merely of the heart, but of daily living in the world; not merely of commitment, but of enactment. It means being so at one with Christ, that the world identifies us with Jesus Christ: that people see Christ in us, and take note.

It was this identity that the early Methodists understood so well.

They applied themselves faithfully to the discipline required to sustain it, which in turn meant that they willingly accepted the guidance and supervision of their class leaders. This combination of intentional discipline and leadership is why Methodism had such an impact on eighteenth century England. The early Methodist societies had members who knew the importance of their task as Christian disciples; and, just as important, they had leaders who knew the business of leading.

AN EARLY METHODIST CLASS LEADER

Fortunately, we have quite a number of records of early Methodist class leaders. Some of these appeared in the *Arminian Magazine*, founded by John Wesley in 1778. Others were published in the nineteenth century from personal letters and journals. One such publication became a spiritual classic, on both sides of the Atlantic: the *Life of William Carvosso, Sixty Years a Class Leader.*[29] Carvosso was a farmer who lived in Cornwall in the west of England from 1750 to 1834. His name reflects the old British heritage of that part of the country, which was also a fertile area for Methodism. He became a class leader in 1774, and in 1814 he retired from farming in order to give all of his time to this work. Indeed, the last twenty years of his life comprise the greater part of his memoirs, compiled by his son, and are rich with spiritual wisdom. Here is one who knew what it meant to introduce people to Jesus Christ, and to help them grow in their discipleship.

We can best illustrate the quality of Carvosso's leadership with excerpts from some of his letters, in which he advises other class leaders how to pastor their class members and how to order their own spiritual lives. Letter writing did not come easily to him, for he was not a well educated man, and did not begin this aspect of his pastoral work until he had retired from farming and was well into his sixties. But he applied himself nonetheless, and became a prolific correspondent, often spending days at a time on his ministry by mail.

The first example is from a letter written in 1826 to a colleague who was also a Methodist local preacher:

> I wish to know how your faith stands, and how you are getting on in the ministry; whether in fishing for souls you have of late been as successful as in former days. I trust the Lord is still with

you, and does not leave you to go warfare at your own charge. How does your little class thrive? Are all the members alive to God? all healthy and strong? all fruitful branches in the heavenly vine? I am afraid that both preachers and leaders too often lose sight of the importance of full salvation. It clearly appears to me, did I lose sight of this, my faith would soon lose its edge. I hope you have not lost your zeal or your love for precious souls; whenever this occurs, our usefulness is all over. . . . I can assure you, that, since my first acquaintance with you, I have not ceased day and night to remember you at a throne of grace. May a double portion of Elijah's spirit rest upon you![30]

As with all his communications, this letter went directly to the point. His concern for souls was a mark of many an early class leader—a concern that went far deeper than whether people "felt at home" in the societies, or were "assimilated" into their fellowship.[31] Class leaders had a burning desire for the very salvation of their members, and an equally pressing concern to shape their discipleship as the fulfillment of that salvation. Carvosso addresses this even more directly in another letter, where he quotes from a sermon he had just read:

"The great salvation of the gospel is communicated moment by moment from above, and is apprehended by simple faith. It is our duty every moment to expect, and our privilege every moment to receive, a full salvation. The act of faith must be repeated till it is ripened into a habit; and when faith in Christ is become the habitual and uniform disposition of the heart, it will secure a constant participation in all the blessings of the new covenant. Our privilege is to enter now into the enjoyment of the salvation we need; and, having once apprehended, never to lose it, but hold it fast unto the end."[32]

There could be no better statement of the nature and purpose of a disciplined Christian life. We do not learn discipleship overnight. We must form habits, and allow the Holy Spirit to change our inward disposition, so that obedience to Jesus Christ eventually becomes instinctive, and disobedience becomes thoroughly abhorrent. Note also that Carvosso, who was seventy-six when that letter was written, was still an avid reader—another mark of the early Methodist class leader.

His pastoral advice by correspondence was increasingly sought in his closing years. In late October 1829 he penned 21 such letters, including this one, again to a fellow class leader:

> My Dear Brother, I wish to know how you and your little flock are getting on; and whether any have strayed from the fold or not "in a dark cloudy day." I trust none of them are lost by your fault or negligence. My prayer is, that all your members may be more and more united in love to one another, and that they may grow up in Christ, their living Head, in all things. . . . Before Jesus, the chief Shepherd, left this lower world, he gave to Peter a strict charge respecting the flock, saying, "Feed my lambs." You will observe, my brother, he calls them, "my lambs;" his own blood-bought property. I have often observed, he first mentions the lambs, because he well knew they would require much care and nursing. But he gave him also a particular charge respecting the sheep, twice saying to him, "Feed my sheep." May the Lord endue you, my respected friend, with all that heavenly wisdom, grace, and understanding, necessary for you to conduct your little flock in safety to the care of the great Shepherd and Bishop of souls above. In due time you shall reap, if you faint not.[33]

Nor did he hesitate to rebuke when necessary, as in this letter to a class leader the following year:

> My Dear Joseph, Soul-work is important work. . . . With respect to visiting from house to house; when you were first fixed as a leader, I know it was your meat and drink to do it; for the salvation of their souls lay near your heart. If they discover less diligence and love manifested toward them in this respect, it is apt to discourage them, and lessen their esteem for their leader. You will bear, I hope, with my plain dealing. It is because I love you that I speak thus. I wish you to look well to those precious souls put under your care; that, in the great day, when you will be called to give an account of your stewardship, you may be enabled to say, "Here am I, lord, and those committed to my care; not one of them is wanting."[34]

It was this directness that gave Carvosso, and so many of these early class leaders, their authority—the authority of those who know they carry pastoral responsibility—the authority of the coal miner described in the Introduction (above, p. xxi). Being *of* the people, they understood the people, and the people understood

them. The spiritual insight they received as the gracious gift of
their office was put to use through familiar language and images.
Carvosso's son, himself a Methodist preacher, pays tribute to this in
the preface to his father's memoirs:

> His illustrations, which told so remarkably, were commonly of
> the most simple kind. He would seize on anything open to the
> senses, and in one way or other render it subservient to his great
> object, the bringing of the soul to Jesus: and his deeply spiritual
> mind, clear conceptions of the subject, and great simplicity of
> soul, rendered this mode of instruction highly interesting and
> profitable.
>
> [On one occasion], entering into the house of a poor man,
> known to him to be deeply and sorrowfully concerned for the
> salvation of his soul, he found him blowing the fire, to assist in
> preparing the ordinary meal. My father said to him, "John, if
> you had half as much faith in Jesus Christ as you have in those
> bellows, you would be at liberty in a moment." This at once
> brought the subject of faith in Christ within the man's reach, in
> an instant he saw—he felt—he believed—and was saved from
> all his sins and sorrows.[35]

A RETURN TO CLASS LEADERS

There are many other records and journals we could cite to show
how class leaders shaped the discipleship of the early Methodist
societies. But these excerpts from Carvosso's memoirs are more
than enough to provide a rich flavor of the office that once gave
Methodism its fiber and its reputation. Suffice it to say that it is
time we bring them back as a vital dimension of our congregational
life and work.

We cannot, of course, reintroduce class leaders in the same form.
Their role was shaped by the conditions of eighteenth century
England as well as by the vision of John Wesley, and much history
has intervened. Moreover, they reached their full potential in the
early nineteenth century on the American frontier, where they
exercised even more pastoral responsibility than in England; and
again, much history has intervened.

Accordingly, if class leaders are to provide us with a contemporary role model for leaders in discipleship, we must take fully into
account not only their historical context, but also the social and

religious context of late twentieth century North America. This is the necessary "homework" of any generation of Christians who wish to learn from their spiritual forebears, and we must not make the mistake of thinking we can take shortcuts. Unlike most homework, however, this will by no means be a chore. For we shall not only find unexpected riches in the past tradition of class leaders, waiting to be rediscovered and reapplied in the church of today. We shall also find the tradition to be alive and well today in some branches of Methodism—a world family of churches that at long last is beginning to acknowledge its common heritage.

FOR REFLECTION

1. In what sense do you understand the church of Jesus Christ to be "one church"? (p. 19)

2. Do you feel affection for The United Methodist Church? For your congregation? (p. 20)

3. Have you ever encountered "a meanness of spirit" and "a party zeal" in your congregation? (p. 21)

4. "Good manners and good taste dictate that, whatever the nature of our call to discipleship, others are not disparaged by our response." (p. 22) Has this ever been an issue for you?

5. Is the concept of *ecclesiolae in ecclesia* real to you, or imaginary? (p. 22)

6. Have you ever experienced the "subtle danger of spiritual self-deception"? (p. 25)

7. Can you think of present-day examples of *bands* and *select societies*? (p. 26)

8. To what extent do church members need disciplinary oversight today?

9. What do you make of "that enthusiastic doctrine of devils"? (p. 32)

10. Would you welcome the pastoral oversight of a William Carvosso today?

Chapter Three
The Class Leader in North America

ACROSS THE ATLANTIC

Strictly speaking, the beginning of Methodism in North America was the visit of John and Charles Wesley to the colony of Georgia in the mid-1730s.[36] The story of this missionary venture has been told many times, and often with the implication that it was a failure, particularly for John. Yet the time they spent in Georgia meant that both brothers retained strong ties with North America, and indeed, both hoped to return. One example of this is the great respect John had for Jonathan Edwards, many of whose writings he republished in England. He also conducted a regular correspondence with Samuel Davies, Edwards' successor as President of Princeton College. Another example is the lasting interest he had in the ministry of George Whitefield, who spent many years as a traveling evangelist in North America, furthering the first "Great Awakening" that had begun in New England. In spite of theological differences with Wesley, Whitefield's efforts to spread "vital religion" identified him with the Methodist movement, and many of the individuals and groups he nurtured in North America were the seed for Methodist societies that were to emerge in the 1760s.

The formation of societies with connectional links to Wesley began during this decade under the leadership of Thomas Webb in Philadelphia, Robert Strawbridge in Maryland, and Philip Embury and Barbara Heck in New York. A number of lay preachers had made their way across the Atlantic by then, but the groundwork of the societies depended much more on class leaders. The nucleus of the first society formed by Robert Strawbridge was a class led by a neighbor, John Evans; and class leaders continued to be a major resource for Strawbridge as he developed societies throughout Maryland and Virginia. By the time annual conferences began in 1773, the system of class meetings had become integral to Methodism in North America, and class leaders were clearly indispensable to their organization.

PASTORAL CONCERN

As in England, becoming a class leader was often the first step toward becoming an itinerant preacher. Leading a class was where one learned to pray in public, and to "exhort" from the scriptures. But above all, this was where one learned the care of souls, the most important responsibility of a pastor. Indeed, in their annotations to the 1798 *Discipline*, Coke and Asbury went so far as to describe class meetings as "our universities for the ministry."[37]

Early Methodist biographies show this to be the pattern time and again. John Emory, for example, who was later to become one of the outstanding bishops of the Methodist Episcopal Church, regarded his class meeting as an essential means of grace from the very beginning of his Christian life. In 1806, not long after his conversion, he was quick to take his fellow members to task when they failed to turn up for a meeting:

> At fifteen minutes after three, p.m., Rev. R. Sparks met the class in Centreville. But few members attended, owing, in part, to the hour of meeting being changed from four to three, without previous notice. This, no doubt, disappointed some, but others, we fear, were absent from want of inclination to be present. Such are inexcusable: how will they be able to give an account of themselves in that day? Are we not commanded to wait in all the means of grace? And is not the deliberate omission of a known duty equally as culpable as the wilful commission of a known crime? Most certainly, for the same God that has forbidden the one has commanded the other. O that God would revive religion in this part of his vineyard, and rouse lukewarm professors [i.e., those who profess faith in Christ] from their lethargic Laodicean security![38]

Clearly, here is a pastor in the making, with a zeal so sensitive that it borders on true spiritual leadership. In another biography from the same period, we find attendance at a class meeting to be life-changing for James B. Finley, who later became a preacher on the Ohio frontier. His account of this experience gives us such a vivid description of a class meeting that it is well worth quoting at some length:

> One day my wife manifested great anxiety to have me go with her to a Methodist prayer and class meeting about six miles distant, but my prejudices were so strong against that people

that I could not think of such a thing. From the various reports I
had heard concerning the Methodists, I believed they were the
worst of all deceivers, and, if possible, they would deceive the
very elect themselves. On my declining she was much affected,
and went out and wept. This scene moved me, and I relented
and told her to get ready, and I would get the horses and we
would start. When we arrived there my presence seemed to
strike all with dismay. I had been so wicked that they had all
given me up to Satan. . . . The general inquiry was, "What has
brought him to meeting?" The time having arrived for meeting to
commence, it was opened by singing and prayer. I conformed to
the rules, for I never was wicked enough, devil though I was, in
the estimation of the people, to persecute the righteous, or show
my ill-breeding and vulgarity by disturbing a worshipping as-
sembly, nor would I suffer any one else to do it where I was
without correcting them. After several prayers, the leader—Mr.
Sullivan—rose and said, "We are now going to hold our class
meeting, and all who have enjoyed this privilege twice or thrice
[i.e. as visitors] will please retire, while those who have not and
are desirous of being benefited by the exercises may remain. My
wife also kept her seat. The members of the class eyed me very
closely, and I could easily tell by their furtive glances that my
room [i.e. my leaving] would be better than my company. The
leader, as is customary on such occasions, opened the speaking
exercises by relating a portion of his own experience, in which he
spoke feelingly of the goodness of God to his soul. After this he
spoke to the rest in order, inquiring into their spiritual pros-
perity; addressing to them such language of instruction, encouragement, or reproof, as their spiritual states seemed to require. It
was a time of profound and powerful feeling; every soul seemed
to be engaged in the work of salvation. I was astonished beyond
all expression. Instead of the ranting, incoherent declarations
which I had been told they made on such occasion, I never heard
more plain, simple, Scriptural, common-sense, yet eloquent
views of Christian experience in my life. After all the members
had been spoken to the leader came to me, and, in a courteous,
Christian manner, inquired into my religious condition. To his
kind inquiries I could only reply in tears and sighs; for I felt as if
my very heart would burst with an overwhelming sense of my
wretched state. Much sympathy was awakened on my behalf,
and many prayers offered to God for my salvation.[39]

Finley spent much of that night in prayer, and the following morning received such an assurance of the Holy Spirit that he was "heard over the neighborhood," shouting and praising God.[40]

CLASS LEADERS IN THEIR PRIME

There could hardly be a more convincing illustration of the importance of class meetings than this testimony from James Finley—and likewise of class leaders. For here was a leader who immediately perceived the crisis in Finley's Christian pilgrimage, and did not hesitate to press him forward, quietly and firmly.

It was in situations such as this on the American frontier that class leaders truly came into their own, more so even than in England. In communities where visits from circuit riders were often few and far between, and where life was rough and ready, these men and women emerged as pastoral leaders of the first order, accepting the care of souls with all of the resonsibility that such a charge required. As we shall presently observe, their prime was relatively short-lived, as was that of the circuit rider. But for at least a generation, lay men and women exercised pastoral leadership in direct succession, not only to the early Methodist movement in England, but also to the early church. And, like their predecessors, they saw the fruits of their labors, and knew they were of the true vine.

LITERATURE ON CLASS MEETINGS

To judge from the many references to class leaders in biographies from this period, it would seem that we should also have a a wealth of literature on the office. Just as in Wesley's England, however, there is little to be found on the subject, except in the *Disciplines* of the church. There is a good reason for this. When class meetings were healthy, and when the office of class leader was being exercised with strength and vitality, there was no need of manuals. Requirements in the *Discipline* and word-of-mouth were sufficient. It was when class meetings began to decline, and when class leaders began to lose their authority in church leadership, that we find books and treatises extolling the virtues and the necessity both of the institution and the office.

Two such books were published in the 1850s, by John Miley in Cincinnati, Ohio, and by Leonidas Rosser, in Richmond, Virginia (for by then the Methodist Episcopal Church had divided between North and South). Both authors make clear that they regarded class meetings and class leaders to be in serious decline; and both exhort their respective churches to revitalize the institution and the office.

Rosser's work is the more substantial, and shows him to have been a keen student of Wesley's writings. Significantly, he regards the class leader as the person primarily responsible for the vitality of the class meeting:

> As Methodism depends to such a vast extent upon the classes for its vigor, simplicity, purity, efficiency, and very being, surely to the same extent the leaders are answerable for the consequences—for the superintendence and guidance of the classes are committed mainly to them. That the classes, in a thousand places, are in a languishing condition, there is no doubt; and that this sad state of affairs is attributable principally to the delinquency of the leaders, there is likewise no doubt.[41]

THE DUTIES OF CLASS LEADERS

Rosser proceeds to expound on the duties of class leaders, stipulated in the *Discipline* of the Methodist Episcopal Church, South, and based on Wesley's own directives:

(1) *To inquire into the inward spiritual state of each class member*. We find no fewer than twenty-three diagnostic questions under this heading, placing a great deal of pastoral responsibility on the class leader.

(2) *To inquire into the outward life of each member, according to the General Rules in the Discipline*. Conformity to these Rules (consisting essentially of Wesley's *General Rules*), "is required as a test of religious character, since they are all contained substantially in the Bible."

(3) *To advise, reprove, comfort, or exhort, as occasion may require*. "In the absence of the pastor, to whom shall a Christian, in spiritual doubts and difficulties, go for advice, but to his leader?"

(4) *To visit the sick members of the class*. The class leader is often "more intimately acquainted with them, than the pastor is or can be." The presence of the leader is especially needed "at the sickbed of the dying saint."

(5) *To inform the minister of any that walk disorderly, and will not be reproved.* "The greater proportion of backsliding in our church is to be ascribed, doubtless, to the want of promptness in the leaders to visit delinquent members."

(6) *To meet the ministers and the steward once a week, in towns and cities, and on the circuits as often as possible.* "Every leader always, when practicable, should be in his place at the leaders' meeting. The Discipline expressly requires it. The duties of his office demand it." [42]

SIGNS OF DECLINE

All of this would read very well, were it not for two significant factors. The first is that both authors spend many pages defending class meetings—a sure sign that the institution was increasingly being criticized by pastors reluctant to enforce weekly attendance on their parishioners. Second, and perhaps more significant, the procedures recommended for class meetings, and the duties enjoined on class leaders, are more appropriate for the disciplined societies of early Methodism than for an expanding church—another sure sign that the office and the institution were in trouble. In fact, the twenty-three diagnostic questions that Rosser provides for class leaders to inquire into the state of their members' souls are even more searching than Wesley's questions for band members. [43] He instructs leaders to ascertain whether all the members "aim constantly at being wholly devoted to God," or whether they "compromise their duty, and keep back a part, though a small part, a very small part." Do they "take up their cross daily? cheerfully? resist the bent of nature, and oppose selfishness in all its insidious forms, and detect it in all its disguises?" Do they "humble themselves in every thing?" Are they "willing to be persecuted for Christ's sake? or to be blamed and despised for doing good?" Do they "seek the entire destruction of inward idolatry, pride, self-will, and impatience?" [44]

Questions such as these may have been asked of society members in the early days of the Methodist movement, and they should have been asked of the class leaders themselves. But as criteria for the membership at large of a growing church, they were spiritually unrealistic. The inference is inescapable. By appealing to the standards of early Methodism, Rosser rendered them idealistic, and thereby confirmed that class meetings and leaders were already in serious decline.

FROM SOCIETY TO CHURCH

To understand this decline, we must begin with an obvious historical fact: In 1784, North American Methodism became a church. Under Wesley's leadership in England, the Methodist societies were part of the Anglican church, "little churches within the big church" (*ecclesiolae in ecclesia*). And, as we saw in the previous chapter, Wesley vigorously resisted any suggestion of separation. In December 1789, not much more than a year before his death, he wrote that any Methodists who would be so "bold and injudicious" as to separate from the church would "dwindle away into a dry, dull, separate party."[45]

Yet in practice, as the Methodist societies grew in numbers and in strength, Wesley allowed their relationship with the Church of England to become increasingly tenuous. Frank Baker, whose *John Wesley and the Church of England* remains the definitive account of this prolonged and often agonizing course of events, identifies some of the "firsts" in the move toward separation: Wesley's venture into open-air preaching on April 2, 1739; his convening of the first annual conference on June 25, 1744; his acceptance of lay preachers as his "sons in the gospel"; and his signing of the Deed Poll in February, 1784, which incorporated the Methodist Conference as a legal entity.[46]

THE MOTHER CHURCH OF METHODISM

The crucial steps, however, were those which he took in response to the events of history in North America. In 1784, having ordained Thomas Coke as superintendent, and Richard Whatcoat and Thomas Vasey as elders, he sent an open letter to the American Methodists in which he declared:

[The] case is widely different between England and North America. Here there are Bishops who have legal jurisdiction. In America there are none, neither any parish ministers. So that for some hundred miles together there is none either to baptize or to administer the Lord's Supper. Here therefore my scruples are at an end: and I conceive myself at full liberty, as I violate no order and invade no man's right by appointing and sending labourers into the harvest.

I have accordingly appointed Dr. Coke and Mr. Francis Asbury to be Joint Superintendents over our brethren in North America: as also Richard Whatcoat and Thomas Vasey to act as elders among them, by baptizing and administering the Lord's Supper.[47]

As is well known, at the Conference held in Baltimore over the Christmas of 1784, The Methodist Episcopal Church in America was officially constituted, making it the mother church of Methodism.

UNCERTAIN IDENTITY

While the actions at the Christmas Conference were very clear, the Methodist Episcopal Church and its successors have always found their identity as the mother church of Methodism difficult to accept. It is rarely claimed, and for that matter rarely acknowledged. There was little doubt, then or now, that the events of 1784 marked a separation from the Church of England. That was clearly understood, not only because of the political climate, but also because of Wesley's ordinations. Where there was ambivalence, however, then and now, was in the transition being made from the identity of a movement within a church to that of an independent church. In the words of Frederick Norwood, Methodists have never really decided "whether they would be a great church or a holy people."[48]

The issues of doctrine and church order in this transition were of course important, and still are.[49] But of much greater importance for the rank and file of the American Methodist societies was the question of discipleship. As a movement within the Church of England, Methodist societies were not only free to develop their spiritual lives. They were also free to be much more disciplined. The *General Rules*, the weekly class meetings, the quarterly examinations and class tickets, all betokened a commitment and a mutual accountability which the average churchgoer would never have contemplated then, and would certainly not accept today. The freedom for this disciplined discipleship lay in the fact that these were not conditions for belonging to the church, but for being a Methodist. One did not have to be a Methodist to retain one's standing in the Church of England, or any other church.

CHURCHLY RESPONSIBILITIES

When Methodism became a church, major adjustments were inevitable. Instead of being a movement within the church, setting the pace for faithful discipleship and congregational vitality, the societies found themselves with institutional responsibilities as well. Not that these responsibilities were thrust on them suddenly. On the contrary, for several decades the rapid expansion of Methodism, especially during the "Second Great Awakening" of the early nineteenth century, seemed to sustain the spirit of Wesley's disciplined discipleship, and even surpass it. As the circuit riders braved the hardships of the frontier, they left class leaders and stewards in charge of the societies they established, and made it their business to fulfill their true call: to proclaim the gospel of Jesus Christ to as many as possible in as many places as possible. The life was hard, and there is no more eloquent tribute than the inscription of a contemporary illustration, "A Methodist Missionary frozen to death in the wilderness."[50]

As the nineteenth century progressed, however, circuit riding gave way to more settled pastorates. In part this was due to the desire of clergy to have a family life, to say nothing of the rigors of traveling on the frontier. But at the same time, settlements were developing into townships, and church members preferred their preacher to reside in the parish, where he and his family could be a more permanent fixture in the community, albeit subject to changes of appointment each year. In due course, this too began to change, as the length of pastoral appointments increased, and congregations began to adjust to a different mode of leadership. This happened much earlier in the east; but by the middle of the century, it was also true of the frontier.

A QUESTION OF LEADERSHIP

In retrospect, it becomes clear that the first half of the nineteenth century provided Methodism with a golden opportunity to forge a shared pastoral leadership between clergy and laity—something that would have reflected the freedom of a new church in a new country, and very possibly been unique in Christian history. Instead, the Methodist Episcopal Church moved inexorably toward a clergy-dominated leadership. In large measure, this was due to the lasting influence of Wesley. Not only did he regard the Methodist societies as part of the Church of England, but he also regarded his leadership of their affairs as a vital and necessary link with the pastoral authority of the church. As we have noted (above, p. 45), the links between Methodism and the Church of England became increasingly tenuous as the movement gathered its own momentum. Yet as long as Wesley remained their spiritual guide and mentor, he insisted on retaining full pastoral authority over the societies. As late as 1790, he wrote to John Mason, one of his assistants: "As long as I live, the people shall have no share in choosing either stewards or leaders among the Methodists. We have not and never had any such custom. We are no republicans, and never intend to be." [51]

Such authority did not always sit well in Wesley's lifetime, still less after his death. There were schisms as early as 1792 in North America and 1797 in England. [52] Yet by and large, the leadership of clergy was readily accepted in North American Methodism. For the first few decades following the establishment of the Methodist Episcopal Church, there was ready collegiality between circuit riders and class leaders, especially on the frontier, where they shared all the toils and dangers of their laity. For that matter, so did their bishops. When it was widely known that episcopal leaders such as Francis Asbury and William McKendree were as much on the road as any circuit rider, if not more, and were receiving the same stipend, leadership that might otherwise have been regarded as authoritarian was accepted as a given, and even as a blessing.

As the nineteenth century progressed, however, and institutional organization developed in conjunction with more settled pastorates, questions of leadership became more divisive. The exclusion of laypersons from Annual Conference sessions, and from the quadrennial General Conferences established in 1808, was a major factor in the formation of the separate Methodist Protestant Church in 1830. Lack of collegiality was also a factor in the stereotyping and formalizing of class meetings, a sure sign that the creativity of class leaders was not being encouraged or motivated. [53] In this respect Rosser was absolutely correct: the health and effectiveness of a class meeting rested squarely with the class leader. What Rosser did not make clear was that class leaders could not merely be assigned such pastoral responsibilities. They also had to know they were trusted to exercise it. Class leaders who were concerned for the work of the gospel and the vitality of their congregations did not seek leadership for its own sake.

AN "UNNECESSARY WHEEL"

We do not have time to chronicle this assumption of pastoral power by the clergy. Suffice it to say that the opportunity to create a vital and collegial working relationship was lost. Norwood suggests that there was an economic factor in this transition. As life on the frontier became increasingly prosperous, congregations could afford to support a full-time pastor. As long as this support had to be shared among a number of appointments around a circuit, class leaders were needed in each place to "perform those pastoral functions which are part of a balanced ministry." But when a preacher became a stationed pastor, supported by a congregation in a parsonage, "the class leader (and along with him, the local preacher and exhorter) became, at least it seemed, an unnecessary wheel." Thus, "inadvertently, because of the settling down of the traveling preacher, Methodism lost one of its strongest supports, the active 'ministerial' participation of the lay people."[54]

AN UNFORTUNATE IRONY

While economics may well have played an important part in this transition of leadership, the literature we have cited, and the various Methodist *Disciplines* throughout the nineteenth century, indicate that the decline in authority of the class leader was by no means inadvertent. Ironically, the very strength of the office in the early Methodist Episcopal Church proved to be a major cause of its demise. We have already noted that many of the early itinerant preachers came from the ranks of class leaders, as in the examples of John Emory and John Finley (above, pp. 40-41). Many more such cases could be cited, proving this to be the rule rather than the exception. This meant that many of the clergy of the new church had personal experience of the office of class leader; and by the same token, those who remained as class leaders knew what it was to have a call to pastoral work in the church very similar to that of a preacher.

This mixture was, and still is, a sure recipe for power struggles in the church. There is only a hair's breadth between the call to strong lay leadership in the church and the call to full-time ministry. As long as class leaders carried extensive pastoral responsibilities, not only did they and the clergy know a great deal about each other's work. They also knew a great deal about each other's call. Thus there were bound to be the tensions that come with a close spiritual relationship. Only with a truly disciplined discipleship could conflict be avoided; and, as we have noted, this was increasingly difficult to sustain in a growing church. More often than not, the issue came down to a very simple question: Who was in charge?

In all fairness, we must concede that this was an altogether legitimate question to ask. In those days, there was considerable sacrifice in answering the call to full-time itinerancy. Stipends were minimal, and living conditions unreliable. Moreover, in answering such a call, there had to be a sureness of purpose that bred strong leadership. It was only natural that the preacher appointed to a pastoral charge or circuit would want to exercise that vocation to the full. The tragedy was that the price of this clergy leadership proved to be the loss of class leaders as a vital component of congregational life and work.

LOSS OF LEADERSHIP

The first legislative acknowledgments of the transition were in the *Disciplines* of the Methodist Episcopal Church in 1864, and the Methodist Episcopal Church, South, in 1866. Neither church went so far as to demean the office of class leader or to devalue the institution of class meetings explicitly. But in effect, that is precisely what they did when both churches ceased to require weekly attendance at class meetings as a condition of membership in good standing. The trend thereafter was predictable and irreversible. Classes and class leaders inevitably became more and more a formality rather than a means of holding members accountable for their discipleship. In 1872, for example, the Methodist Episcopal Church discontinued disciplinary examination of class leaders each quarter, and incorporated instead the following paragraphs:

The design of the organization of classes and the appointment of Leaders is:

1. To establish a system of pastoral oversight that shall effectively reach every member of the Church.
2. To establish and keep up a meeting for social and religious worship, for instruction, encouragement, and admonition, that shall be a profitable means of grace to our people. . . .

The primary object of distributing the members of the Church

into classes is to secure the sub-pastoral oversight made necessary by our itinerant economy. In order to secure this oversight:

1. Let a report of the condition of his class be presented by the
   Leader at each meeting of the Quarterly Conference.
2. Let each Leader be careful to inquire how every soul of his
   class prospers; not only how each person outwardly observes the rules, but how he grows in the knowledge and
   love of God. . . .[55]

In spite of the injunctions to ensure observance of the rules and
to foster growth in the knowledge and love of God, it is clear in
these paragraphs that the class leader's disciplinary role had been
modified to one of mere pastoral concern. The language of subse-
quent *Disciplines* for both churches became increasingly programmatic and utilitarian until, as we have noted, the office was
deprived of any disciplinary recognition at the uniting Conference
in 1939 (see above, p. xv and n.3).

DISPLACEMENT OF THE CLASS MEETING

Just as the evolution of settled pastorates tended to displace
the pastoral authority of the class leader, so the evolution of the
Sunday school tended to displace the pastoral accountability of the
class meeting. According to The Methodist Sunday School Union,
founded in 1827, the purpose of Sunday schools was the instruction
of children and young people in knowledge of the Bible and in the
service and worship of God."[56] But in the latter part of the nineteenth century, adult classes began to emerge as part of the "self-
culture" movement generated by Bishop John H. Vincent and
others.[57] Originally designed for the training of teachers, these
classes soon developed their own momentum, as adults saw how
much they too could learn about the Bible, and much else besides.
With the development of new publications aimed at their particular
interests, they soon became an established part of congregational
life.

The agenda of these adult Sunday school classes was very different from that of the older class meetings, and far less demanding in
terms of accountability for one's discipleship. They provided learning, not discipline; and they fostered freedom of discussion, not
the following of rules. On both counts, they were more appealing
than the older class meetings, many of which had by then become

hardened in their ways and stilted in their leadership. Since both Methodist Episcopal Churches had already determined in the 1860s that attendance at class meetings was no longer a requirement for church membership (see above, p. 50), it was clear that adult Sunday school classes would eventually replace class meetings; which, after the turn of the twentieth century, they did.

THE QUESTION OF SLAVERY

There is one further factor to be taken into account in the decline of the class leader, and as research continues into this period of Methodist history, it may well prove to be the most critical factor. It is the issue of slavery. The Christmas Conference of 1784 had adopted some very specific injunctions regarding the emancipation of all slaves held by Methodists, and had even specified a timeline.[58] But the following year, all of this legislation was tabled for further discussion; and thereafter, any decisive action on the issue was evaded.

There were many who continued to campaign vigorously for abolition, and the various General Conferences continued to deplore slavery, to some extent providing a check on slave dealing.[59] But the moral and ethical imperatives remained rhetorical, until the agenda of the nation as a whole made confrontation unavoidable. The facts are well known: a major separation over the issue with the formation of the Wesleyan Methodist Church in 1843; and the following year, the agreement of the Methodist Episcopal Church to divide into two churches, North and South. This division not only rendered slavery a matter of mere opinion. It also helped to set the course of the nation toward civil war.[60]

LOSS OF INTEGRITY

The issue for Methodist leadership is the extent to which this compromise disempowered clergy and laity alike. Could a church disregard the teachings of Jesus to this extent and retain any integrity in its ranks for accountable discipleship? The answer is self-evident in the tortuous arguments that raged throughout Methodism, North and South, as the nation became increasingly divided.[61] There can be no other conclusion: The Methodist Episcopal Church came under God's judgment following the division of

1844—the part of the church that insisted on separation, and the part of the church that allowed it.

The question can well be put the other way: Whether a church committed to a strong collegiality between clergy and class leaders would ever have been caught up in such a compromise. For to render a moral issue such as slavery subject to social and cultural pressure was to remove Christ from the center of its congregational life. Whereas, had clergy and class leaders sustained their collegiality in the task of forming Christian disciples, their concern for obedience to Jesus Christ would perforce have confronted them with his teachings, and may well have convinced them more directly of the sin for which North American Methodism has subsequently done much to atone, but for which it has yet to repent.

The lesson is clear, and sobering. As we recover the office of class leader for the church of today, we may well be confronted with the risen Christ in ways that surprise us, discomfort us, and call us to a discipleship that proves costly. These chapters of our history should be explored. They still have much to teach us, painful though the instruction might be.

KEEPING THE TRADITION ALIVE

As we have already noted, the decline of class leaders and class meetings did not mean that they disappeared entirely. Two very fine books on class leaders were published by John Atkinson (1882) and Charles Goodell (1902), indicating a continuing tradition in the Methodist Episcopal Church. Both books display sound scholarship and eminently practical guidelines. Atkinson, for example, identifies six necessary attributes of class leaders: a working spirit, blamelessness, common sense, intelligence, sympathy, and enthusiasm. He also urges class leaders to direct their members toward service in the community, especially toward the poor.[62] Goodell suggests a metaphor for class leaders that may grate on late twentieth century sensitivities—"the Drillmaster of Methodism."[63] This is by no means unhelpful, however, and is included in Chapter 5 as one of the images that can help define the office for today.

Goodell also provides some powerful biographical vignettes of late nineteenth century class leaders, indicating that, in spite of the trend in the church, there were still places where class leaders continued to serve the church in the forming of Christian disciples. It is clear, however, that by the turn of the century such leaders were not being replaced in the Methodist Episcopal Churches. Goodell's book was essentially a valediction.

AFRICAN AMERICAN METHODISM

Where the tradition was really kept alive was in the African American branches of Methodism: the African Methodist Episcopal Church (A.M.E.), the African Methodist Episcopal Zion Church (A.M.E.Z.), the Colored Methodist Episcopal Church (after 1954, the Christian M.E. Church [C.M.E.]), and also in the African American conferences of the Northern church. There were some social and economic reasons for this, as F. Herbert Skeete observes:

> The need for the class leader of course was different in black Methodism. Lack of sufficient numbers of black preachers meant that the circuit plan continued as a vital part of the operation in the CME, AME, and AMEZ Churches, and in the black Conferences of the parent body. Further, black pastors often had to take time out for secular employment to supplement the meager support of their churches. . . . So partnership with the laity in the work of the ministry was a necessity for the black church. Unlike the white church, the class meeting and the class leader continued to be crucial.[64]

However, social and economic reasons alone do not explain the role of the class leader in the African American tradition. As Skeete further points out, class leaders and class meetings gave people who were being denied their proper place in society an opportunity to develop their spiritual potential. People who were "still in a difficult phase of social and economic development" found the spiritual support of class meetings "an indispensable part of their church life—an instrument of mutual pastoral care."[65]

Thus, even though African American Methodists likewise went through the transition from society to church (the A.M.E. Church being founded as early as 1816), their racial oppression left them with social and economic needs that continued to be met through the class system. This meant that they also retained the spiritual benefit of this system, which helped to keep the discipleship of the African American church much more integral to the worldly living of its members. For them, the church was and is a giver of hope, "as an emotional cathartic, as a center of community activity, as a source of leadership, and as a provider of respectability."[66]

AN EXTRACT FROM A.M.E. POLITY

A good example of this can be found in the Polity of the African Methodist Episcopal Church, written by Bishop H. M. Turner in 1885. His comments on class leaders grip us, even today:

They should be of deep personal piety, mature experience, ability to give religious counsel and advice, wisely and affectionately, and to influence the members, young and old, to the systematic charge of their Christian duties. They should be well versed in the Discipline of the church, daily readers of the Bible, sufficiently familiar with the Holy Scriptures to apply the Word of God to the varied cases of every person they may lead. They should read the lives of the persons eminent for piety; commit to memory the sayings of holy men of all ages, the better to become acquainted with the different shades of experience and the Christian duties devolving upon the church. They should be good singers, and should have from twenty to forty hymns committed to memory; should . . . observe family prayer at their homes, and see that their children attend both Sabbath-school and public preaching, and they themselves, regularly. They should . . . attend the house of God forenoon on the Sabbath, and worship when all nature lends a helping hand, and not wait till Sabbath night to bestir themselves, when the owls, bats, coons, frogs and other animals, which are afraid of light, creep forth from their dark retreats. They should also be polite, mild in expression, accustomed to speaking to the members, not gossippers, news-carriers, haughty, light, triflers and given to too much joking, but on all occasions should be grave and venerable.[67]

While this clearly echoes another century, it is a powerful and vivid piece of writing, imparting not only the respect in which the office of class leader was held, but also the spiritual authority of those who held it. Moreover, while it might seem daunting to those of us considering the reintroduction of the office today, and might even make us wonder whether we will ever find such persons, a careful reading of Bishop Turner's criteria reveals that there is little here which might not be reasonably expected of any church leader—then and now. If the list reads abrasively, it is because we have too long sought leadership in the church that leads us nowhere at all. It should also be noted that this *Polity* was considered worthy of a new edition in 1986, including the passage just cited.

AFRICAN AMERICAN UNITED METHODISTS

The office of class leader has also been kept alive in many African American congregations of The United Methodist Church. A good example of this is Salem United Methodist Church, in Harlem, New York City. The congregation was first organized in 1902, and from the outset made the system of classes and class leaders an integral part of its congregational structure. The system has been consolidated over the years by each of its pastors, two of whom have been elected to the episcopacy: Roy C. Nichols and F. Herbert Skeete. Some of the classes have as many as 200 members; others are much smaller in size. But each has a class leader who is appointed on the recommendation of the pastor and approved by the administrative board. Leaders such as Ruby Pate and Annie Springer carry a considerable pastoral workload, and are entrusted with a great deal of responsibility. They are also accorded much respect, and not without good reason. As Bishop Skeete observed when he was senior pastor:

> I have found more dedication and commitment [among class leaders] than one usually finds even among the clergy. We have one leader who has been faithful in his service for over 45 years. During that time, he has been mugged, robbed, and attacked in his travels to and from the discharge of his Christian duties as a leader. Yet he keeps on going in spite of increasing difficulty and danger to his health.[68]

Another African American congregation that continues the tradition of class leaders is St. Mark's United Methodist Church in Montclair, New Jersey, where Violet Goodwin and Russell Morgan, Jr. coordinate twenty-two classes, each with a leader and co-leader. St. Mark's has developed its own Class Leader Training Guide, compiled by Violet Goodwin and Ernest S. Lyght, who was then the pastor of the congregation. Bible study is an important feature of this class system, with recommended readings for each quarter. Guidelines are also provided for the development of skills among the class leaders, who meet regularly in a Class Leaders' Council. The stated objectives of the class leaders at St. Mark's include providing the pastor with information about members who need pastoral calls, identifying the spiritual needs of individual families, and developing accountable discipleship through witnessing and pastoral attention to every member.[69]

OTHER METHODIST TRADITIONS

There are other Methodist churches around the world where the tradition of class leaders and class meetings is alive and well. We have room here only for a sampling. In Africa, class meetings have not only continued, but have thrived in a number of countries. Norman Thomas notes that, in South Africa, women's fellowship groups, known as *Manyanos*, are subdivided into classes, each with a class leader who receives special training, and is elected by the Leaders' Meeting. They must be persons who "have spiritual feelings and sufficient Christian experience, must know the scriptures, and show a fruitful life."[70] In Zimbabwe, women's groups known as *Rukwadzanos* are likewise patterned after the class meeting. Each year they hold an outdoor revival meeting attended by up to 10,000 persons.[71] And in the United Kingdom, where class leaders all but disappeared earlier this century, there are places where the office is being revived with great pastoral effectiveness.

In other parts of the world, the tradition of class leaders is being revitalized by the introduction of covenant discipleship. In the Uniting Church of Australia, where the historical research of Gloster Udy and the pastoral interpretation of John Mallison have long fostered a renewed tradition of small group discipleship, the New South Wales Synod has adopted covenant discipleship as a feature of its missional outreach, due in large measure to the leadership of Dean Drayton, Director of Missions, and his staff colleague, David Nash.[72] In the Fijian Methodist Church, the tradition of class leaders is being revitalized under the guidance of the Christian Citizenship Secretary, Finau Tu-uholoaki, who also introduced covenant discipleship to the curriculum of the Davuilevu Theological College in 1987. At the Methodist Seminary in Bergen, Norway, many of the students have taken part in covenant discipleship groups, with the supportive example of teachers such as Tore Meistad and Roald Kristiansen. And the original handbook for the groups, *Accountable Discipleship*, has been translated into German by Helmut Nausner, superintendent in Vienna, for use by the Methodist Church in Austria.[73]

There are also some bold new experiments. In the Concepción District of the Methodist Church in Chile, the Superintendent, Osvaldo Herreros, has incorporated the principles of covenant discipleship and class leaders into a project for evangelistic outreach among the Mapuche and Pehuenche Indians. And in El Paso,

Texas, David Chavez has adapted covenant discipleship groups for evangelistic outreach and community building, incorporating some of the principles of the *comunidades eclesiales de base* of Latin America.[74]

THE KOREAN TRADITION

A branch of Methodism that merits special mention is the Korean Methodist Church, where class leaders and class meetings have been integral to its organization from the earliest days of Methodist missions more than a century ago. In 1986, there were 35,000 organized Methodist class meetings in Korea, with 300,000 regular class members, and a publication for class leaders with a circulation of 65,000, in a church of just over a million members. Since then there has been much additional growth, attributed in large measure to the outreach of these classes into the community, and the pastoral effectiveness of their class leaders.[75] Nor is this limited to Methodism. The Yoido Full Gospel Central Church in Seoul, said to be the largest congregation in the world, is organized into "cell groups" very similar to the class meeting.[76]

The great majority of Korean American immigrant Methodist churches in the United States have brought the class system with them. For the most part, the classes meet in the evenings in people's homes—though not always weekly, due to distances and schedules. Hae-Jong Kim (see above, p. xv) perceives these classes to have four implications for the life and work of Korean immigrant congregations: worship, fellowship, discipleship, and stewardship.[77] But he also stresses that they are part of the pastoral ministry of the congregation, and not a separate movement. "Even the class meetings in Korea, which are mostly led and taught by lay people . . . are used as extended arms of the pastor. The pastoral oversight and supervision is a very important factor. The class leaders are directly accountable to the pastor. . . . [It is in this sense] that laity participates in 'pastoral' ministry."[78]

The importance of continuing and developing the office of class leader in North American Korean congregations is recognized by The United Methodist Church in the appointment of its national staff. The portfolio of the Rev. Heisik Oh, editor of Korean language resources in the Division of Church School Publications of the General Board of Discipleship, includes the preparation of materials for use by classes and class leaders.

MUTUAL LEARNINGS FROM
A COMMON TRADITION

At a seminar to launch the revitalization of class leaders through-out The United Methodist Church, held at Nashville, Tennessee, in May 1991, one thing became very clear. As we proceed to recover this uniquely Methodist office, we shall have much to learn from the various traditions that now comprise the Methodist family of churches. United Methodist congregations in the African American tradition, such as Salem and St. Mark's, as well as Korean immigrant congregations and our sister denominations, the A.M.E., A.M.E. Zion, and C.M.E. Churches, can all provide us with the best possible teachers—class leaders who are still "on the job." Just as important, we can all learn together from the originative Wesleyan tradition. We might even become "Methodist" again.

FOR REFLECTION

1. "Becoming a class leader was often the first step toward becoming an itinerant preacher" (p. 40). Since most congregations no longer have class leaders, how do preachers take this "first step" today?

2. Have you ever experienced "a zeal so sensitive that it borders on true spiritual leadership?" (p. 40)

3. When class meetings were healthy, there was little need of manuals (p. 42). Can you think of other such examples in the life of the church?

4. Do you find the duties of class leaders listed by Rosser to be spiritually idealistic? (pp. 43-44) Why, or why not?

5. Have you ever thought of the Methodist Episcopal Church as "the mother church of Methodism"?

6. Do you find the church of today clergy-dominated?

7. Has your congregation ever experienced a conflict between the leadership of clergy and laity? How was the conflict handled?

8. From what you have read thus far about class meetings, do you perceive them to be different from Sunday school classes? Or are they similar?

9. In what ways do you think that the risen Christ is likely to surprise and discomfort us today? (p. 53)

10. Does the language of Bishop Turner grip you? (p. 55)

Chapter Four

Recovering the Tradition of Class Leaders

TRADITION AND TRADITIONING

The purpose of our study thus far has been to explore the heritage of Methodism to see if we can recover the office of class leader for the church of today. This sounds fairly straightforward, but in fact it is quite a complicated process. And since we are now at the point where we must apply our findings, we need to clarify where we have been and where we are headed.

The technical words for what we are doing are *tradition* and *traditioning*. Both words, the noun and the verb, have Latin origins. The verb *to tradition* means to hand down, or to hand over; the noun *tradition* refers to a saying or teaching that is handed down or handed over. As with most words that are used by theologians and church historians, they are not part of our day-to-day Christian vocabulary. Indeed, they are a good example of what John Wesley meant when he said he preferred "plain truth for plain people," and that he labored to avoid "all words which are not . . . used in common life; and in particular those kinds of technical terms that so frequently occur in bodies of divinity, those modes of speaking which men of reading are intimately acquainted with, but which to common people are an unknown tongue."[79]

While this is sound advice in general, there are nonetheless some technical words with which church leaders, both clergy and laity, need to be familiar—words that greatly expand our understanding of the gospel and help us to foster a more faithful Christian discipleship throughout the church. *Tradition* is such a word. As a verb, *to tradition* the gospel means to hand on to others the good news of Jesus Christ, so that each generation of Christians can know it for themselves and live it out as faithful diciples. "Traditioning" the gospel also means handing it over to each generation of human beings in the world, so that they too may hear the

61

good news of salvation in Jesus Christ and be invited to come home to the family of God.

As a noun, the Christian "tradition" is first and foremost the gospel itself: the good news brought to us by Jesus Christ, and the good news about Jesus Christ proclaimed by the early church. This tradition was committed to writing by the early church, and edited to form the New Testament which, along with the Hebrew Bible, is the definitive record of God's salvation in Jesus Christ, and thus the ultimate authority for any traditioning of the gospel.

The Christian tradition also includes the history of the church. As with anything that has been traditioned for this length of time, the Christian tradition has been enriched by the knowledge and experience of many generations, and has also had to withstand much mischief. The witness of countless Christians across the ages must therefore be traditioned along with that of the early church. They too have honored Christ. Their faith, their faithfulness, their wisdom, their actions, and their methods can help us with our discipleship today—if, that is, we will include them in our traditioning.

FAITHFUL TRADITIONING

Christians who are faithful in traditioning their tradition thus have a great deal of work to do. First, they must receive the tradition from the preceding generation of Christians. Then they must apply themselves to understanding it in light of the scriptures, the authoritative written account of the tradition. Then they must ask what other generations of Christians have done with this tradition: how they have understood it and lived it out in their own day and age; what lessons we have to learn from their experiences, their trials, and their errors.

Having done all of this, Christians must then ask what they themselves can do to appropriate the tradition for their own day and age: how they can apply its truths to their own lives; how they can make it a message of good news for the world in which they live; how they can embody this message in a faithful discipleship that is truly a sign of God's love, peace, and justice in the world; and how they can ensure that the tradition is handed on to the next generation in faith and hope. The imagery in the Letter to the Hebrews is vivid. Those who have completed their laps are cheering us on—and expecting us to run our laps with no less vigor and determination (Heb. 12:1).

THE PRESENCE OF THE RISEN CHRIST

All of this may seem an impossible task for those of us who live ordinary Christian lives. After all, not everyone can be a full-time student of Christian tradition. But in fact, traditioning is exactly what we do in our congregations and in our daily Christian living in the world. In our worship, in our programs, in our outreach, and in our service, we are traditioning the tradition of the gospel—making it relevant for the world in which we live, and shaping our lives around its central truths.

We cannot, of course, take all, or even most, of the credit for this. The reason we are able to do it at all is that none of it is done in our own strength. For the gospel is not just a human tradition. It is centered on the risen Christ, who is present in the person and power of the Holy Spirit. The task of receiving the gospel, appropriating it, living it out in the world, and handing it over to the world, does not therefore ultimately depend on human ideas and values. It depends first and last on a loving obedience to the Christ in whose name we have our faith and hope. In other words, it depends on our discipleship.

THE METHODIST TRADITION

For well over 200 years, Methodism has been an important part of the Christian tradition. As we have seen in the last two chapters, the early Methodist societies, and then the various Methodist churches, developed their own traditions, appropriating the gospel in distinctive ways, and making their particular contributions to the Christian tradition as a whole. Most especially, Methodists have traditioned the gospel for the world. Methodism has been nothing if not missional and evangelistic.

As we observed, class leaders have always been a vital dimension of Methodist traditioning. From the very beginnings of the Methodist movement, class leaders played a pivotal role in receiving and appropriating the gospel, handing it on to the members of their classes, and making sure they handed it over to the world. Indeed, their role in traditioning the gospel was so important that their very office became part of the Methodist tradition. Class meetings were the genius of Methodism; and the key to the class meeting was the class leader.

A DETRADITIONED OFFICE

Unfortunately, as we also observed, the office became seriously detraditioned. In the mother church of Methodism, now The United Methodist Church, it has lapsed entirely in the great majority of congregations. Not that the picture is altogether gloomy. There are branches of Methodism where class leaders have been retained. Moreover, thanks to faithful Korean traditioning, they have been restored to The United Methodist *Book of Discipline* (above, p. xv). But if we wish to reinstate the office across The United Methodist Church of today, the task that faces us is no longer one of traditioning, but of *re*traditioning—that is, recovering the tradition.

RETRADITIONING THE OFFICE

While this presents a serious handicap, it also provides an opportunity. The absence of class leaders today in most United Methodist congregations means that we can retradition the office without having to deal with the mistakes of previous mistraditioning. We have an opportunity to revitalize the office with a clean slate, so to speak, yet with much on record from which to learn, and with colleagues from other Methodist traditions from whom to seek advice.

We began this process of retraditioning in the preceding chapters. We first turned to the Bible, and saw how this pattern of leadership was present in the ministry of Jesus himself (Chapter 1). Then we looked at the origins of the office among the early Methodists, and saw how they found it indispensable to their discipleship (Chapter 2). We noted how Methodists of other generations traditioned, and then detraditioned the office in their own day and age—though with some notable exceptions (Chapter 3). And now we come to the critical point of retraditioning: how we can appropriate the office for the church of today.

If we do our traditioning carefully, we will not try to transfer the office of class leader from another time and place in history. Rather we will trans*plant* it. We will shape the office for our own day and age, and firmly plant it in the context of contemporary congregational life and work. The class leaders of today may well emerge with a different job description from that of their English and

American forebears. But their identity will be the same: leaders who are commissioned by the congregation to help their fellow church members be better witnesses to Jesus Christ and more obedient followers of his teachings in the world: in short, to help them be faithful disciples.

THE UNITED METHODIST CHURCH AND ITS CONTEXT

To do this, our next step must be to take stock of The United Methodist Church and its cultural context. This is not to say that other Methodist churches, or other denominations for that matter, cannot undertake a traditioning of class leaders for themselves. But in what follows we shall be traditioning the office primarily for United Methodist congregations. Others may then draw their own conclusions from what we discover, and apply these findings to their own situations.

We can begin with the two contextual observations we made in the Introduction:[80]

1. The North American church is very much part of the North American culture.

Church life in the United States of America is integral to North American culture; and in turn, North American culture greatly affects the church. Statistics alone tell us this, in that some three quarters of the nation claim affiliation with denominational Christianity.[81] And in spite of some notable attempts to forge a distinctive identity, as in the recent volume *Resident Aliens* by Stanley Hauerwas and William Willimon,[82] most North American Christians consider the church to be part of their national heritage rather than the place where the gospel of Jesus Christ is traditioned and where they learn how to practice faithful discipleship.

However we might evaluate such a state of affairs, it is a contextual reality. We must therefore keep very much in mind that we are dealing with a church that does not have the characteristics of early Methodism, on either side of the Atlantic, nor yet of other Methodist traditions worldwide. The great majority of congregations in The United Methodist Church are firmly in and of the late twentieth-century U.S.A.

2. The culture of contemporary North America is individualistic and consumerist.

In spite of general concern about the weakening of community life, North American society remains persistently individualistic and consumerist. This trait is reinforced by the technologies of mass communication and mass production, all of which are designed to meet individual needs. The church tends to reflect this aspect of the culture far more than challenge it, which means that many persons who come to church primarily out of a sense of spiritual need find themselves confronted with an array of programs and activities designed to meet social and cultural needs more than the development of their discipleship. This in turn means that congregations tend to focus more on those aspects of the Christian life that are fulfilling rather than on those that are demanding; whereas true Christian discipleship, as we have noted (above, p. 5), calls for weighty obligations and costly service along with its considerable benefits. The circle is a vicious one and shows little sign of being broken.

A COUNTER-CULTURAL OFFICE

Since the office of class leader is designed to foster obedience to Jesus Christ through a community of faith and a life of service in the world, it is certain to run counter to this cultural context. Rather than address people's social and personal needs, class leaders will call them to Christian accountability. And while this will ultimately address their deepest need of all—the need to be back in the family of God where they belong—it will not always and everywhere be well received. Indeed, it is likely to meet resistance at many points. The fact that there are admirable precedents for this, not only in Methodism, but also throughout Christian history, will not make the task of class leaders any easier.

The resistance can be lessened, however, if our retraditioning of the office takes into account these cultural factors. Provided we are careful to appropriate the essence of how class leaders originally functioned, and are likewise careful to keep the office faithful to the teachings of Jesus Christ, we shall find it stimulating and rewarding to adapt it for the church of today. Most church members are yearning deep down for genuine leadership in discipleship, and they will welcome it from persons who truly care for the flock (Jer. 23:1-4).

CAREFUL TRADITIONING

This is why our traditioning of the office must be done with great care. On the one hand, the cultural pressures of our North American context will tempt us to adopt class leaders merely as a means of providing better pastoral service to a church membership already well blessed—a temptation we must steadfastly resist. This is not to say that persons with genuine pastoral needs should be neglected; but the office of class leader must make a clean break with the cultural consumerism that the North American church so readily reflects and so seldom questions.

At the same time, if class leaders are to be effective in the church of today, we must take fully into account that The United Methodist Church is a large, inclusive religious body, broadly representative of North American society—in fact, the equivalent of the Church of England in Wesley's day. We must also take into account that the pastoral leadership of the church has been firmly in the hands of clergy for a number of generations. Strong lay leadership in this area has not only not been developed: it has often been discouraged.

THE IMPORTANCE OF THE PASTOR

For all these reasons, it is vitally important for clergy to be involved from the outset in the retraditioning of class leaders. The pastor of the congregation is the person to whom the spiritual welfare of the flock has been entrusted, and who is ultimately responsible for the discipleship of each member. If he or she has no understanding of the office of class leader, and no appreciation of what it can accomplish, there is little point in beginning the process.

Such a lack of understanding, however, will rarely be the case. If the pastor is reluctant to consider class leaders, it is more likely to be due to a healthy caution. Our present vacuum of leadership in discipleship has produced numerous programs and strategies over the past few decades, each designed to revitalize congregations and revive church members. It is understandable, therefore, that a pastor might hesitate to move too quickly in yet another new direction. If this is the initial reaction of your pastor to the idea of class leaders, be patient. Ask for some time to discuss the concept in some depth. Suggest forming a group of interested persons to explore the implications, without any pressure of commitment. Let the process of traditioning work as it is meant to work—by grace.

In point of fact, you are much more likely to find that the pastor of your congregation is very interested in the idea. Far more pastors than we might imagine are ready to share leadership in the forming of Christian disciples. Pastoring the entire congregation has become very burdensome in the consumerist culture we have just described. Many church members have come to expect very personal service from their pastor, and are quick to express disappointment and disapproval when their expectations are not met. Others are unwilling to accept the leadership skills that pastors have spent many years acquiring. To share these pressures and frustrations with trusted lay colleagues, and to enter into a collegiality of spiritual leadership, might be just what your pastor is ready to do.

FIRST THINGS FIRST

Once the interest and support of the pastor have been secured, there is still much to be done before the class leaders can be appointed. In fact, if the foundations are to be well laid, preparations will take several years. This may sound excessive; but we must remember that it took the Methodist Episcopal Church more than a hundred years to detradition class leaders, and the ground for their retraditioning must therefore be thoroughly prepared. A congregation reintroducing this office is considering much more than a program, but a leadership role that will foster a return to the very roots of Methodism.

Not least of the reasons for such careful preparation is that class leaders will bring a major change to the way our congregations are pastored. They will give our members a more intentional leadership in discipleship than they have known in a long time, if ever they have. The "spiritualized discipleship" so common today among North American Christians (see above, p. 31) will be called into question. Not only will this mean cultural resistance from a consumerist-oriented church membership, but it will also require class leaders to have good credentials for their office. They will have to be seen as leaders—persons who are actually leading the way—and the congregation will have to learn to accept them. A period of several years is not at all too long to prepare everyone for these adjustments.

A CLIMATE OF ACCOUNTABILITY

If class leaders are to fulfill their potential in the forming of Christian disciples, congregations will have to be receptive to their leadership. And for this to happen, church members must begin to understand Christian discipleship as a lifestyle rather than as a mindset. Following the teachings of Jesus Christ in the world must be given priority no less than believing in him. Walking with Christ must be no less important than talking with him. If the work of class leaders is to be effective in our congregations, there must first be a climate of accountability.

The reason for pressing this point is once again the cultural context of the North American church. In our prevailing climate of consumerism, anything offered or proposed by church leadership tends to be assessed in terms of its benefits. Many members join the church for precisely this purpose, and many congregations recruit new members with precisely this inducement. If class leaders are introduced without clear indication that they are about some very different business, with some very different priorities, they will be regarded as yet another programatic initiative to make church life more enriching, and their call to accountability will be viewed merely as an option.

COVENANT DISCIPLESHIP

There is no better way to nurture such a climate of accountability than through the implementation of covenant discipleship groups, or something very like them. These groups are also a traditioning of the Methodist tradition, in that they adapt the early class meeting for the church of today. Consisting of up to seven persons, they meet for one hour each week, and hold themselves mutually accountable for their discipleship in light of a covenant which they themselves write. The companion volume, *Covenant Discipleship* (DR091B), describes how to introduce and develop these groups.

If your congregation is contemplating the introduction of class leaders, and there is no tradition of accountability among the membership, begin with covenant discipleship. The groups will draw together the potential leaders in discipleship—persons who are ready to "go professional" in their Christian lives (see above, p. 16); and once the groups are functioning, they will also provide role models in discipleship for the rest of the church membership.

They will be seen to be accountable for their walk with Christ in the world, and this in turn will help create the necessary climate for class leaders.

It takes at least two years for covenant discipleship groups to become established in a congregation. They are first introduced through a pilot process that takes one year, following which the entire church membership is invited to join. The response is usually around 15 percent of the average Sunday morning attendance, or 5-7 percent of the membership roll. These new groups then require a further year in order to find their feet and create a firm place for themselves in the life and work of the congregation.

While all this is happening, groundwork can also be laid for introducing class leaders (see Part 3 of the companion volume, *Forming Christian Disciples*). But it cannot be over-emphasized how important it is to foster this climate of accountability first. If your congregation already has covenant discipleship groups in place, or some other form of accountability, well and good. Provided there are persons who are attending regularly to the teachings of Christ by "watching over one another in love," and are seen to be doing so, then you have the necessary foundation for class leaders. If not, then the introduction of the office will be premature until you have done something about it. Jesus himself took several years of careful preparation to develop the first disciples as leaders of the church; and throughout the writings of John Wesley we find countless references to the same careful preparation of class leaders.

THE GENERAL RULE OF DISCIPLESHIP

One of the most significant ways in which covenant discipleship groups develop a climate of accountability is in the writing of their covenants. These are not put together haphazardly, merely reflecting the strengths or preferences of the members. They are written according to some clearly defined guidelines, based on the teachings of Jesus and drawing on the *General Rules* of the early Methodist societies. First published by Wesley in 1743, these *Rules* went through thirty-nine editions in his lifetime, indicating that they were very widely used.[83]

By traditioning the *General Rules* for the church of today, covenant discipleship groups have developed a "General Rule of Discipleship" to shape their covenants:

To witness to Jesus Christ in the world,
and to follow his teachings through
acts of compassion, justice, worship, and devotion,
under the guidance of the Holy Spirit.

This General Rule holds in balance the components of a faithful discipleship. First there is the honoring of Christ as savior and sovereign. Then there is intentional application to his teachings, a fourfold obedience that acknowledges him as prophet no less than priest. And lastly, there is an openness to the power and presence of the Holy Spirit.

It may seem that this General Rule is an attempt to legislate discipleship. On the contrary, since each group writes its own covenant, there is always flexibility in how it is applied. Moreover, it is a very general rule. The guidelines are basic, merely holding members accountable for a lifestyle that is not in their own hands, but rather in the hands of Christ. And, as we noted in Chapter One, the teachings of Christ are very simple indeed. We make them complicated only when we are trying to tailor them to our own needs and preferences—or worse, are trying to avoid them altogether.

EXTENDING THE GENERAL RULE

It is the responsibility of class leaders to extend the General Rule of Discipleship throughout the congregation. Needless to say, this does not mean prevailing upon all church members to join covenant discipleship groups. We have already observed that these groups are intended primarily to develop a climate of accountability in the congregation. Only 5-7 percent of church members are ready for this form of commitment, and any attempt to impose covenant discipleship on the congregation as a whole would certainly fail—just as most of the Church of England in Wesley's day was unwilling and unready to join Methodist societies.

Even if not to this degree, however, most church members today are willing to be accountable in some measure for their discipleship. Whatever their motives for joining a congregation, they took membership vows openly and honestly, and they are often disappointed that more is not required of them once they are part of the church. By the same token, they are often puzzled by the lack of basic guidance in how to live as Christians in the world. It is all very well to have the freedom to respond to God individually, but much of the time they find it difficult to discern what God wants them to do. The fact of the matter is that many church members badly need some guidelines for their Christian living. And even if they chafe a little at first, they will welcome the General Rule of Discipleship as a fixed bearing in a world awash with conflicting values and priorities.

The task of the class leader is to provide church members with just such a compass heading: a witness to Jesus Christ in the world that is confirmed by acts of compassion, justice, worship, and devotion, while still allowing for the freedom of a spiritual relationship with God. Members will respond to this Rule in different ways, because their walk with Christ will be at different stages. But two things are sure: We badly need direction for our discipleship; and we need trusted leaders who will hold us to our course.

CLASSES AS PASTORAL GROUPINGS

Class leaders fill this role by accepting basic pastoral responsibility for *classes* of church members. These classes are not the same as Sunday school classes, nor are they convened as class meetings. They are rather in the nature of pastoral groupings, consisting of fifteen to twenty persons who receive guidance and support from a class leader in living out their discipleship according to the General Rule. Suggestions for assigning the classes are provided in the companion volume, *Forming Christian Disciples*, the most important of which is that each class should be broadly representative of the congregation as a whole. The last thing a class should be is a grouping of "problem" members, or "inactives," or those with special needs.

One of the first priorities of a class leader is to get to know his or her class, and Chapter 6 explores this task in some detail. In many instances, however, the members of a class will already be known to the leader, and the task will not be as formal as it sounds. What will be different is the relationship, and this will have a clear purpose: To provide the class members with help and encouragement in the basics of their discipleship. As the relationship develops, the class leader will become a trusted friend. But the friendship will be a firm one, because it will always be directed toward an accountability for faithful discipleship.

"TRACKING THEM DOWN"

This was powerfully illustrated for me some years ago at a district meeting I was invited to address in New York City. After I had made my presentation, an older woman identified herself as a class leader. She belonged to an African American congregation where the office had been faithfully traditioned, and she gave us a description of how she set about her duties. She was still active as a class leader at age 79!

"I have fifteen people in my class," she began, "and eight of them come to church every week. I don't have to worry about them. I have a quick word on Sunday morning, make sure they are attending Sunday school and Bible study, and are not getting into any trouble. But the other seven," she continued, "they're something else. They need more looking after. They might have problems at home that need my advice. They might have problems at work they need to talk about. They might need help in resisting the pressure of the streets. And they might also need a friendly push in the direction of church—because we all get lazy from time to time. In other words, I have to track them down." She paused with dramatic effect. "And I get them!"

Everyone had a vivid picture after her eloquent testimony. This old saint would spend hours getting to the homes of these absentees, probably changing buses several times, and almost certainly risking violence in the streets (see above, p. 56). But when she arrived and knocked on the door, it was the good shepherd tracking down the wayward sheep. There would be love and concern in the question, but also a firmness: "And where were you on Sunday?"

We need this kind of firmness if we are to have faithful Christian disciples in our congregations. Pastors cannot provide it. They don't have the time. And even if they did, they don't have the peer relationship with church members that brings true friendship with firmness—the knowledge that the class leader who is concerned about accountability is also a fellow church member, facing the same challenges and the same pitfalls of Christian living in the world. The early Methodists practiced this kind of friendship by "watching over each other in love," and we will experience it once again in our congregations as we retradition the office of class leader. We will no longer be playing at discipleship. We will be practicing the real thing.

WHY NOT CLASS MEETINGS?

All of this brings us back to the question of why we should recover the office of class leader without bringing back class meetings at the same time. Was it not in class meetings that the early Methodists "watched over each other in love"? And is not the value of small group meetings for mutual support well demonstrated today in many other aspects of congregational life and work? In those branches of Methodism where class leaders have continued to function, class meetings have usually continued as well, particularly in the Korean tradition. And covenant discipleship groups, already advocated in this chapter as a preparation for class leaders, are an adaptation of the early class meeting. Would it not further assist class leaders in their work if their classes met together rather than have the leader contact each member individually?

We considered some of these questions in the Introduction (above, pp. xvii-xx), where we suggested that this may well happen in due course. Just as it quickly became clear to the earliest Methodist classes that coming together every week would not only be more convenient for their leaders, but also a pastoral advantage for themselves, it may also become clear to these new discipleship classes that a time of weekly fellowship would be a significant means of grace. But we must remember that the early class meetings were groups of men and women whose disciplined commitment was far from that of the average church member of today. They agreed to abide by a very specific set of rules. They submitted to a quarterly examination in order to keep their membership in good standing. They attended their weekly class meetings, not only as a means of grace, but also as a condition of membership. They were "little churches" within the church, and not at all representative of the rank and file parishioners of the eighteenth century Church of England.

To the extent that The United Methodist Church is the equivalent of the Church of England in Wesley's day, we cannot expect this disciplined lifestyle from the average church member. But we can, indeed we should, expect it from the leaders of the church, both clergy and laity. This has been the purpose of traditioning the early class meeting as covenant discipleship groups for the church of today—a means of leadership development. Perhaps, by grace, we shall have a similar accountability across the entire church. But first, we must establish leaders in discipleship who can begin to extend the General Rule of Discipleship to pastoral groupings of church members. These discipleship classes may become class meetings; but only when they are ready.

A "NEW FRONTIER"

All of this means that the new generation of class leaders in The United Methodist Church will be pioneers, defining their office as they exercise it. They will have much in common with their Methodist forebears, but they will also be breaking new ground. To borrow a phrase, they will be on a "New Frontier," engaging in what Lesslie Newbigin has termed a "missional encounter" with Western culture.[84] In addition to careful traditioning of their office, therefore, they will need contemporary images to shape their self-understanding. The following are just a few examples of how class leaders can be re-imaged for the church of today. Hopefully other images will emerge as the office takes its place again in the structure of the church. As with all metaphors and analogies, these images have limitations. They should be regarded as explanatory illustrations, not as strict models or paradigms.

THE CLASS LEADER AS COACH

One way to describe the role of a class leader is by likening it to that of a coach; not in the sense of a head coach of an athletics program, as the word is often used today, but rather of a person who helps to improve basic skills in a particular area. The relationship with a coach is bound to be personal, because of the nature of the coaching. But the focus of the relationship is the particular skill one wishes to improve, whether it be in sports, music, preparation for an academic examination, or any other area.

The relationship between a church member and a class leader is likewise concerned with improvement—in this case in the basics of Christian discipleship. It too is a personal relationship, but it is focused on a relationship that is ultimately far more important. For the agenda of class leaders is to show their class members how to deepen their relationship with Jesus Christ: how to follow his teachings more faithfully in the world; and how to practice the spiritual disciplines that keep them open to the grace and power of the Holy Spirit.

THE CLASS LEADER AS DRILL INSTRUCTOR

This is an image that has to be used very carefully in connection with the work of the church. Christians have rightly become cautious about anything that seems to advocate war in service of the Christ who came to bring peace on earth. Yet the discipline *per se* of military life has much to commend it, and can readily be applied to Christian discipleship (Eph. 6:10-17). We saw in the previous chapter that one of the last major books to be published on class leaders drew precisely this analogy.[85] Besides which, there are other areas of teamwork in which discipline is necessary, and in which drill instructors or their equivalent play a pivotal role: display teams, for example, or orchestras and choirs.

Wherever teamwork is necessary, drill instructors are indispensable. They are the ones who take novices and make sure they grasp the basic disciplines of the team, or who show existing team members new routines. In learning to march, it is the drill instructor who will show that the left foot is different from the right, and if need be will insist on hours of "marking time" before the squad is ready to move forward. In a display sequence, it is the drill instructor who will walk the team through the basic movements. In an orchestra or choir, it is the section leader who will ensure that the instrumentalists or vocalists have grasped the rudiments of the music.

By the same token, in a congregation it is the class leader who accepts responsibility for grounding church members in the rudiments of Christian discipleship. The very word has the same root as "discipline," and this is precisely what a class leader helps other members to grasp. There are certain basics to a Christian lifestyle; and if these are ignored, or dismissed as unimportant, a congregation's discipleship lacks both form and substance.

THE CLASS LEADER AS GUIDE

Another image for the class leader is that of a guide in discipleship. Just as a drill instructor gives the command to march forward once the squad is in step, and just as an orchestra will ultimately perform under the section leader who has drilled them in practice, so a class leader provides guidance for class members in living out their discipleship in the world. We noted in Chapter 1 that this does not consist of expert advice. That too may be necessary, and can be provided by the specialized ministries of the church. What the class leader provides is something more basic and straightforward: hands-on guidance in walking with Christ—leadership by example.

The image of guide is helpful in identifying the class leader as a fellow traveler in the Christian life, who shares the same journey, with the same hills and valleys, the same obstacles and accomplishments, the same disappointments and satisfactions. Yet a guide is also someone who accepts the responsibility of walking one step ahead, to show the way, and to share some of the practical knowledge that comes from an accountable discipleship. Of course, it is Christ who is the only true leader of Christian disciples. But we often experience that leadership through trusted guides.

THE CLASS LEADER AS CO-PASTOR

With the image of co-pastor, we move from analogy to reality, in that class leaders do indeed share pastoral responsibility for the congregation. The term used is *co-pastor* rather than *sub-pastor*, not because of any intent to reduce the authority of the pastor or inflate that of the class leader, but to allow both pastor and class leaders to fulfill their respective offices more effectively. The line of authority is quite clear in the *Book of Discipline*: Class leaders are accountable to charge conference and work under the supervision of the pastor.[86] Yet there are distinctive areas of pastoral oversight that quite naturally fall to one or the other.

To begin with, class leaders can perform pastoral duties that would not be a good use of the pastor's time. In the same way that a coaching staff works with a head coach, or section leaders work with an orchestra conductor, class leaders can work with the pastor in taking care of basic pastoral oversight. Not only are they just as effective as the pastor in this area; they are probably more effective, in that many of the day-to-day problems Christians encounter in the world do not require expert pastoral counseling, but rather the advice, and often merely the ear, of a trusted colleague or companion. Class leaders can assume these duties quite readily, once the congregation understands and accepts their role.

This in turn frees the clergy for those pastoral duties that only an ordained person can perform, and which tend to be neglected when the pastor is occupied with less specialized tasks. The ministries of word and sacrament are entrusted to ordained clergy because they require intensive study and disciplined application—

precisely what is so often lacking in the lives of many pastors today, as they struggle with the routine pastoral oversight that class leaders could so readily provide.

WHY CLASS LEADERS?

There may well be an objection at this point. Why should this co-pastoring role require the revitalization of an office that the church phased out many years ago? Have not other forms of leadership taken their place just as effectively? Do we not have administrative and programmatic structures that afford the same opportunities for lay leadership? And besides, if the office was detraditioned, perhaps it was for a good reason. Maybe the responsibility of forming Christian disciples proved to be too demanding for laypersons. If so, how much more burdensome will these responsibilities be in a culture that leaves people with very little spare time. In fact, will we find anyone willing to be a class leader?

The answer to these questions lies in the nature of both Christian discipleship and congregational life. If the purpose of a congregation is to develop faithful disciples, then leaders in discipleship are absolutely essential. For without the hands-on guidance of other laypersons, church members are left with only vague concepts and principles for Christian living in the world. As we noted in Chapter 1 (above, p. 14), however inspiring and sensitive professional staff might be, and however well they might organize and administer the church programs, they are always going to be one step removed from where ordinary church members live and work. A congregation will not develop faithful disciples unless there is a strong complementarity between clergy and laity in pastoral oversight.

This is not happening in many of our congregations. Pastoral responsibilities are usually handled by professional staff; and when leadership responsibilities are delegated to laypersons, they are usually in connection with program and administration. By contrast, the office of class leader carries the clear mandate to lead in Christian discipleship. Class leaders will have a unique access to other church members. They will accept responsibility for other church members as no other church official is able to do, with the exception of the pastor. Indeed, they will often be better placed than the pastor to motivate and encourage discipleship among church members, because they will be leading by example. And while the church of today might not be ready for the depth of spiritual leadership provided by the earliest class leaders, the office will always have that potential—a potential we may yet see retraditioned in our lifetime.

A FOUNDATION AND A CATALYST

As the persons responsible for grounding church members in the basics of Christian discipleship, class leaders can be foundational to our congregations. They can demonstrate how the General Rule of Discipleship maintains a balance among the various dimensions of the Christian life, so that undue time and energy are not given to one aspect of Christ's teachings to the neglect of others that are just important, if less comforting. They can show church members how not to confuse spiritual promptings with personal preferences, nor high ideals with the servant work of Christ in the world.

They can also show church members how to acquire the disciplines of the Christian life in the best possible way: by *practicing* them. They can make clear that discipleship is formed, not as a mindset, but as a lifestyle; that the love of Christ is not professed in words alone, but in deeds; that faith becomes not merely a spiritual communion with God, but a walk with Christ in the world; that the anointing of the Holy Spirit is in order to take good news to the poor, sight to the blind, release to captives, and freedom to the oppressed (Luke 4:18). Class leaders can do all of this, and more, if their office is retraditioned in our congregations.

Class leaders can also be catalysts for the ministry and mission of the church. As they help their class members with the General Rule of Discipleship, everyone will see more clearly how God shapes lives for service in the world. At the same time, as they come to know the life and work of the congregation as a whole, its collective gifts and graces—including those of their class members—they will come to know the needs of the community at large. And because the focus of their office is discipleship, rather than program or administration, they will be able to bring all of these diverse factors together in ministry and mission. They will be a means of centering the congregation on Jesus Christ and opening its work to the Holy Spirit.

Class leaders can further be a catalyst for the coming reign of God, since they are the ones who best know how to connect the ministry and mission of the congregation with the world. They know the talents of their members, and they know the needs of people in the community. They will often bring the two together.

HEARING THE CALL

If you have read this far, and the office of class leader has impressed itself upon you as a unique and vital contribution to the forming of Christian disciples, God is probably calling you to do something about it. There may be much preparation before your congregation is ready to proceed, but it can begin with you. As you read on, therefore, be open to the further prompting of the Holy Spirit. You may be one of those who will help to recover the tradition of class leaders.

The remaining chapters provide suggestions and guidelines for pursuing such a call: how to recognize it, answer it, and follow it through by accepting and fulfilling the office of class leader. If this is where God is calling you, you will experience the highest privilege in life other than that of knowing and serving Jesus Christ: You will be privileged to help others to know and serve him. Like the very first disciples, you will help to pastor the flock of Jesus Christ, and through them, the larger family of God.

FOR REFLECTION

1. "There are some technical words with which church leaders, both clergy and laity, need to be familiar" (p. 61). Do you agree?

2. Can you think of examples of "traditioning" in your family and community, apart from your church?

3. Have you ever belonged to a congregation with class leaders? Or with people who fulfill the office under another name? Or who do so without any recognition?

4. Do you agree that the North American church reflects an individualistic and consumerist culture?

5. Have you encountered "lifestyle discipleship" and "mindset discipleship?" (p. 69)

6. Have you ever considered rules for your discipleship?

7. What is your reaction to the General Rule of Discipleship? (p. 71)

8. Do you agree that we need more firmness today in our congregational leaders? (p. 73)

9. Is Lesslie Newbigin correct in calling for a "missional encounter" with Western culture? (p. 75)

10. Which of the images for class leaders do you find helpful? (pp. 75-77) Or unhelpful?

Chapter Five

Discerning the Call: Preparing for the Task

THE INWARD CALL

Your call to become a class leader will come in two ways: outward and inward. While both of these are important, it is the inward call that will eventually determine whether or not you accept the office. And, as with any inward call from God, you are the one who must ultimately discern it.

The most common sign of an inward call from God is a quiet persistence. We can all remember the story of the boy Samuel, and how God called him when he was lying down in the temple. At first he thought it was the priest Eli who was calling him, and three times he arose and went to the old man, only to be told that it was not Eli who had called him. Finally Eli realized it was God who was calling the boy, and told him that next time he heard the call he should say, "Speak, Lord, for your servant is listening" (1 Sam. 3:2-10).

Of course, not many of us actually hear anything when God calls. Most often we experience a sense of unease, or restlessness, gradually leading to a conviction that we need to move in a particular direction or take a particular course of action. At its most critical, the call leaves us with a clear certainty that we have no way out: We must follow this sense of conviction, quite simply because there is nothing else we can do about it. Until we reach that critical certainty, or more accurately, that critical surrender, God's spiritual "promptings" or "nudges" are quietly persistent, disturbing us and leaving us unsettled about where we are and what we are doing. We get no peace of heart or mind or spirit until we respond.

These spiritual promptings may come from any number of sources. We may receive them during our times of personal devotion, through prayer, or Bible reading, or reflection. We may experience them during worship. A hymn, or a sermon, or an anthem may speak to us very directly—as, indeed, may a time of silence.

We may find ourselves newly aware of God's presence in an act of service to someone, as we realize that we have been an instrument of grace in a very special way. We may also find ourselves empowered to be a means of God's justice, speaking words that we never thought we could utter, and realizing that God has very particular work for us to do. The promptings may also come to us through trusted Christian friends, who give us new insights and new assurances—or perhaps new challenges and new questions for our discipleship. In all of these ways, God's Spirit can prompt us, nudge us, persuade us, pester us, and finally confront us with a call.

The call to become a class leader will be no different. Perhaps the preceding chapters of this book have identified a restlessness in your discipleship, and have brought into focus the need for you to take another step in your walk with Christ. Perhaps you have been concerned, as many laypersons are, about the need for some basic leadership in our congregations. You know that young people who are growing up in the church need to be made more aware of their identity as Christian disciples, and that new members need to be shown how to follow Christ with purpose rather than merely by personal preference. Or perhaps the concept of class leaders is causing you to face questions about your own discipleship you have never considered before, but which, now they have been raised, will not go away. All of these promptings and nudgings should be recognized for what they are, and given the appropriate response: "Speak, Lord, for your servant is listening."

THE OUTWARD CALL

In addition to these inward promptings, there are outward ways in which you will receive your call. In all likelihood, the first of these will be an invitation from your pastor to consider the office. If your congregation has followed the procedures suggested in the companion volume, *Forming Christian Disciples*, the decision to introduce class leaders will have been taken by a charge conference, and your pastor will have attended a special seminar sponsored by the General Board of Discipleship. These seminars take place on seminary campuses in the late spring, and invitations are extended to prospective class leaders during the following summer months. You can, of course, be asked at any time; but it is likely to be during the summer.

Besides the pastor's invitation, there is the further outward call of your appointment as class leader by the fall charge conference of your congregation. Before the vote is taken on your appointment, you will be asked to make a short statement, describing your call and your commitment to the duties and obligations of the office. In this way, not only the pastor but the congregation as a whole confirms you and accepts you in this leadership role. And finally, on Covenant Sunday in January, you will be publicly commissioned during morning worship.[87]

In other words, while your inward call is critical, you are not left with the full burden of discerning that this is what God wants you to do. Others have an opportunity to help you recognize your call, answer it, and then fulfill its obligations. Moreover, as your congregation goes through the preparatory steps toward implementing class leaders, you may well receive other forms of affirmation from fellow church members that help to convince you. The office is badly needed in the church of today, and you may be surprised how many people urge you to accept it.

A GOOD REASON TO HESITATE

Even so, you might hesitate to accept the call, and for a very good reason: You do not feel worthy. As you consider the responsibilities of leading other people in their walk with Christ, you realize they are considerable, not least because other church members will be looking to you as an example and a role model. While this does not require you to be an expert in the Christian life (see above, p. 16), it does require you to be faithful. It means you can no longer please yourself in your discipleship. The person you must now devote yourself to pleasing is Christ, and Christ alone.

A sense of unworthiness is therefore altogether appropriate as you consider the call to become a class leader—appropriate because it reflects the truth. Of course you are unworthy to lead others in their discipleship. We all are unworthy. As any teacher or instructor will readily verify, there is no more penetrating self-evaluation than the task of sharing what we know with others. Their curiosity, their questions, and their eagerness to acquire new learning, expose in a very bright light our own lack of knowledge and our own lack of dedication.

The same is going to be true of the office of class leader. If we are to help other church members with their discipleship, we are going

to have our own walk with Christ revealed in a searching light—if
not to others, then certainly to ourselves. As we share the General
Rule of Discipleship with others, we are going to see where we
ourselves have failed to live it out. As we impress on others the
importance of witnessing to Jesus Christ, we are going to realize
how seldom we ourselves have witnessed to him. As we stress the
balance between acts of compassion, justice, worship, and devotion, we are going to see how little we ourselves have done to
follow any of these teachings, still less keep them in balance. And
as we encourage others with the promise of the Holy Spirit to
enable and empower them in their walk with Christ, we will come
to see how spiritually threadbare we are in our own lives. This is
why the apostle Paul could write to Timothy, his "child in the
faith," that he, Paul, was the "foremost of sinners" (1 Tim. 1:2,15).
How much more is that true of each of us.

A GOOD REASON NOT TO HESITATE

Yet Paul also explained to Timothy why this sense of unworthiness had not held him back in his work as an apostle:

> The saying is sure and worthy of full acceptance, that Christ
> Jesus came into the world to save sinners—of whom I am the
> foremost. But for that very reason I received mercy, so that in
> me, as the foremost, Jesus Christ might display the utmost
> patience, making me an example to those who would come to
> believe in him for eternal life (1 Tim. 1:15-16).

In other words, Paul's very unworthiness was an opportunity for
Christ to be honored. Here was someone who had once persecuted
the church, yet who had been called and empowered to be one of
the apostles of Jesus Christ. The mercy and the grace of God were
all the more in evidence, demonstrating that it was not in his own
strength that Paul was an ambassador for Christ (2 Cor. 5:20), but in
the power and love of the Holy Spirit.

The same will be true of you as a class leader. Any guidance you
are able to give a fellow church member, any support, will not
come from you, or even from your gifts and graces. It will be a
work of the Holy Spirit, flowing through you with love and power,
and using your gifts and graces. It will be up to you to allow this to
happen, as you order your life in accordance with Christ's teach-

ings, and as you shape your discipleship around the General Rule. But it will be primarily a matter of getting out of the way of the Holy Spirit—and, just as often, of not getting in the way. There is no question that you are unworthy for such a task. But your very unworthiness is an opportunity for Christ to demonstrate how much can be done with so little.

As you consider answering the call to become a class leader, therefore, you should not hesitate on the grounds of false modesty. This is no less an error than false self-confidence. Of course there are responsibilities to the office, and of course you will have to make some changes in your life in order to fulfill them. But the responsibilities will not be beyond your ability, because they will not depend on your ability. You will not find yourself out of your depth because you will not be swimming on your own. Your first and only responsibility will be to open yourself to the grace of God by following the teachings of Jesus Christ, simple teachings, straightforward teachings. As you do so, you will find that the Holy Spirit empowers your discipleship in spite of yourself. It will not be you leading, but God who dwells in you (1 John 4:13-16).

SEEMINGLY IMPOSSIBLE STANDARDS

In spite of this assurance of grace, you may still doubt your capacity for this sort of office. What is more, you can probably make a good case. The scriptures appear to support you, with all sorts of injunctions about faithful discipleship that seem to set quite impossible standards. You can point, for example, to the contrast Paul draws between the "works of the flesh" and the "fruit of the Spirit" (Gal. 5:19-23). While fornication, impurity, licentiousness, idolatry, sorcery, drunkenness, and carousing might be out of your ballpark, you could certainly plead disqualification on grounds of strife, jealousy, enmities, anger, quarrels, dissensions, factions, and envy—and even more, your lack of love, joy, peace, patience, kindness, generosity, faithfulness, gentleness, and self-control.

You can further support your case with similar injunctions in Wesley's writings. Take, for example, his sermon, "Catholic Spirit," in which he argues for an openness between Christians, a generosity of spirit that will allow for differences of opinion on the nonessentials of the faith. The condition of such a "catholic spirit," however, is agreement on the essentials of Christian discipleship, which Wesley states in the form of some very daunting questions:

Is thy heart right with God? Dost thou believe [God's] eternity, immensity, wisdom, power, justice, mercy, and truth?
Dost thou believe in the Lord Jesus Christ?
Dost thou "know Jesus Christ and him crucified"?
Art thou, through him, "fighting the good fight of faith, and laying hold of eternal life"?
Is thy faith . . . filled with the energy of love?
Does thy soul continually "magnify the Lord, and thy spirit rejoice in God thy saviour"?
Art thou employed in doing "not thy own will, but the will of him that sent thee"?
Dost thou point at him in whatsoever thou dost?
In all thy labour, thy business, thy conversation? Aiming only at the glory of God in all?
Does the love of God constrain thee to "serve" him "with fear"?
Art thou more afraid of displeasing God than either of death or hell?
Is thy heart right toward thy neighbour? Dost thou "love as thyself" all . . . without exception?
Do you "love your enemies"? Is your soul full of goodwill, of tender affection toward them?
Do you love even the enemies of God?
And do you show this by "blessing them that curse you, and praying for them that despitefully use you and persecute you"?
Do you show your love by your works?
While you have time, as you have opportunity, do you in fact "do good" . . . to neighbours or strangers, friends or enemies, good or bad?
Do you do them all the good you can?[88]

Once again, these seem to present quite impossible standards for those of us who try to be faithful disciples in the world of today, still less leaders in discipleship. If you wish to disqualify yourself on grounds of personal inadequacy, you would seem to have a foolproof argument. The issue, you might say, is not false pride, nor yet false modesty, but merely whether the blind should lead the blind. Since clearly none of us measures up to what Paul called the "fruit of the Spirit," or what Wesley described as "having a right heart"; indeed, since none of us can claim to have fully obeyed the commandments that Jesus himself identified as the greatest of all—that we should love God with all our heart, soul, mind, and strength, and our neighbor as ourselves (Mark 12:29-31)—then it would appear that one disciple can do as well or as badly as another. Why not let individuals work out their own walk with Christ?

THE MOST IMPORTANT QUESTION

If you try to use this argument to avoid becoming a class leader, you overlook the most important question for the Christian disciple. The issue is not whether these standards are possible, but whether they are what a Christian *aims* for. Are these the qualities, is this the lifestyle, that you as a Christian would *like* to have?

In some oral traditions of Methodism, there is a deeply moving invitation in the service of Holy Communion. When all has been prepared, and the people are ready to come forward, the pastor declares: "This table is open to all who love the Lord Jesus Christ, or would like to do so." In other words, those who love Jesus Christ are welcome to dine with him. Those who are not sure whether they love him, but know for certain they would *like* to, are just as welcome.

In this simple but dramatic turn of phrase, we find the essence of Christian discipleship. It is not a question of how much we love Jesus Christ, or of what we accomplish or fail to accomplish for him. It is much more a question of *intent*. Jesus knows better than anyone the limits of our faith and our works alike. We do not believe as we should, we do not trust as we should, we do not behave as we should, and we do not serve our neighbor as we should. But the point of declaring ourselves to be his disciples is that we *try* to do these things for him. And that is good enough for Jesus.

It should also be good enough for us. We have spoken a great deal in the preceding pages about the dangers of a discipleship that focuses on our relationship with Christ to the detriment of our obligation to follow his teachings. But this time-honored Methodist invitation to the Lord's Supper leaves us in no doubt all that the ultimate meaning of Christian faith is indeed a relationship with Jesus of Nazareth. We must not cheapen it through careless discipleship; nor must we demean it with self-justification. Our best *is* good enough for Jesus.

HE DID THE BEST HE COULD

This was memorably illustrated for me when I was a schoolboy in England. Each summer, the students would challenge the faculty to a cricket match. It was a popular event, mainly because the students always won. While there are some similarities between cricket and baseball, there are many differences, and this is not the place to explain them. Suffice it to say that both games are played with a bat and a hard ball, and the object in both games is to hit the ball out of reach of the fielding side in order to score runs.

One summer, we were all surprised and delighted to find that our Latin teacher was on the faculty team. He was almost a caricature of the classical scholar: thin, stooped, balding, and with very thick glasses. His nickname was "Crusty," and the less charitable of us referred to him as a walking example of a question mark. When he came out to bat there was general mirth and cheering, and his performance lived up to all our hopes and expectations. He hit the ball only once; several times he threw himself to the ground to avoid it; he ran at the wrong time, causing another member of the team to be forced out; and he failed to run at the right time, costing the side a couple of runs. When the game was finally over, he was greeted with yet more sarcastic cheering.

Later, we asked one of the teachers who coached the cricket team why Crusty had been in the line-up at all. Had the faculty set out to lose the game? Had Crusty really wanted to risk the fast balls hurled at him by students who couldn't believe their luck? The reply we received had much wisdom, and it has stayed with me over the years. "We were short a member, and we asked him to play. He told us he was no good, but that he would do the best he could. And he did. You can't ask a person to do more than that."

Each one of us could probably tell a similar story, and some of us could tell it about ourselves. It illustrates a very important truth about life in general, and about Christian discipleship in particular. Since no one can be accomplished at everything, and few of us become really accomplished at anything, we must do the best we can with the talents that we have. "Crusty" was a very good Latin teacher. Had he been a good cricket player as well, he would have been exceptional. The point was, he was willing to take part in a match where he knew he would probably look ridiculous. As a result, and with the wise explanation of our coach, he grew in our estimation—because he did the best he could.

THEY DID THE BEST THEY COULD

The genius of the early Methodists is that they understood discipleship in this way. They did not lower their sights by reducing the commandments of Jesus to what they thought they could accomplish. Rather, they accepted his teachings as their standard, and set about *trying* to follow him. Of course they knew that their accomplishments would be less than perfect: that their obedience would be inconsistent; that they would stumble and backslide; and that from time to time they would even make shipwreck of their faith. But as long as they did not compromise their *intent* to be faithful disciples, they knew that Jesus would honor their efforts, and that the Holy Spirit would give them the grace and strength to continue. They did the best they could.

If you are hesitating to accept the office of class leader because you don't feel qualified, the most important question to ask yourself is not whether you feel adequate for the job, or whether you think you can measure up to the standards of faithful discipleship. The question is much more basic. Never mind how well you think you are doing in your discipleship, or how badly, is following Jesus Christ what you really *want* to do? If the answer to this question is yes, then your best will be good enough for Christ.

What is more, you will be helping some of your fellow church members who likewise want to do their best as Christian disciples, but feel that their faith is inadequate, or the task is beyond their abilities. Through your work as a class leader, you can reassure them that their best is indeed good enough for Jesus, who understands their strengths and their weaknesses better than they themselves.

READY TO GO PROFESSIONAL

Before we leave the subject of discerning your call, it may be helpful to return to an image that we used in Chapter 1. We talked there about amateurs and professionals, and suggested that the difference between the two is neither money nor skill, but commitment (above, p. 16). Professionals accept full responsibility for the task in hand, and will stand by their work when it is finished. Indeed, good professionals will be embarrrassed by shoddy work, and will do their best to correct their mistakes. Amateurs, on the other hand, always have an excuse. They can shine on a good day, but on a bad day they can always plead, "I'm only an amateur."

We suggested that a great many Christians see themselves as amateur disciples. When they are faithful to Jesus Christ, well and good. But when they let him down, they are quick to plead amateur status. After all, they argue, the standards are so high. Not everyone is meant to be a saint. And provided we forgive everyone else for their weaknesses, God will forgive us for ours. We are sinners, living in a sinful world, and no one is perfect. What more can be expected of us?

Professional disciples, by contrast, make it a point of honor to stand by their work for Jesus Christ. They may be no more accomplished than the amateurs, but their work is reliable and consistent, and their relationship with Christ is constantly developing. Instead of making excuses for their failures and weaknesses, pleading that they are sinners in a sinful world, they do something about it. Instead of talking about what they ought to be doing for Jesus, they get on with the job, even if their performance and their attitude leave much to be desired. And at the end of the day, they have something to show for it, as Jesus made very clear in his parable of the two sons. The question was not which son agreed to work in the vineyard, but which one actually did what the father requested (Matt. 21:28-32).

If you have reached the stage in your discipleship where you are ready to "go professional," to be accountable for your discipleship; and if, regardless of your performance, you are ready to stand by your *intent* to follow Jesus in the world, then you are also ready to be a class leader. The example you set for others will lie, not in your accomplishments or your expertise, but in your commitment and in the consistency of your efforts to follow his teachings. The most influential people in our lives are not the superstars, however much they may inspire us with their feats. The people who really motivate us and move us forward are the people quite close to us, who show us what it is like to try something in life, and who demonstrate that it is possible to do it.

Class leaders are such persons, and if God is calling you to the office, you must answer for the simple reason that the church desperately needs your service in this area of leadership. Yes, the office will bring much additional responsibility, and yes, many burdens. But Jesus Christ cannot shepherd your congregation without your help; still less can your pastor. Your own concerns must ultimately be set aside, and you must consider only this: You are needed.

PREPARATION THROUGH
COVENANT DISCIPLESHIP

We have already stressed the importance of covenant disciple-ship groups, or some other form of mutual accountability, as a means of preparing the congregation for class leaders, and as a place where their leadership can be developed (above, p. 69). A further word now needs to be said about covenant discipleship as a preparation for the office, and as a condition of holding it.

If you are already in a covenant discipleship group, you will know how this helps to form your walk with Christ: how the cove-nant your group has written keeps you accountable for witnessing to Christ in the world, and for following his teachings through acts of compassion, justice, worship, and devotion; and how the shar-ing of your discipleship with trusted Christian friends heightens your sensitivity to the promptings and warnings of the Holy Spirit. Most especially will this be the case if you use the *Covenant Disciple-ship Journal* to record your discipleship week by week.[89]

The longer you have been in a group, the more you will also have come to experience the truth of that phrase in Wesley's *General Rules*: "watching over one another in love." You will have come to value these weekly times of deep Christian communion, and to understand more fully what Jesus meant when he said that "if two of you agree on earth about anything you ask, it will be done for you by my Father in heaven. For where two or three are gathered in my name, I am there among them" (Matt. 18:19-20).

As you answer the call to become a class leader, you will further realize how these weekly meetings have prepared you to lead others in their discipleship. By holding yourself accountable week by week, you have come to understand that following Jesus Christ in the world is first and foremost a matter of obedience—disci-plined obedience. The famous violinist, Isaac Stern, has said that only discipline frees the artist to let talent and imagination take wing. Only by practicing scales does the musician have the free-dom to play a concerto. Only by running laps does the athlete keep fit for the race. Only by practicing the basic teachings of Jesus Christ is the disciple free to be creative for the coming reign of God in the world.

This is the most important learning you can impart to others. The members of your class may well surpass you in the richness and imagination of their accomplishments for Christ. They may have five talents to your two. So be it. What they can learn from you is how to use those talents, how to apply them in service to God and their neighbor. The accountability you practice week by week will be an example for them, and also a means of grace. You will show them, with whatever gifts and graces God gives you, how to walk with Christ, consistently, reliably, and obediently.

A CONDITION OF THE OFFICE

If you are not in a covenant discipleship group, and you have been asked to accept the office of class leader, you should join a group as soon as possible (see the companion volume, *Covenant Discipleship*). Indeed, belonging to a covenant discipleship group will be a condition of the office as long as you hold it.

Far from being an officious requirement, or implying that you lack integrity in your walk with Christ, this condition merely exercises the common sense of our Methodist forebears. Quite apart from the advantages it affords you in personal preparation for your work as a class leader, membership in a covenant discipleship group gives you important credentials in the congregation. You are seen to be holding yourself accountable for your discipleship, and thus to have something significant to share with others. By the same token, not everyone in your group is going to be a class leader, and this will give you the opportunity to be in regular contact with church members who are "professional" disciples like yourself. Your meetings with them will be free of the responsibilities of class leading, so you can focus on your own accountability week by week. Their support, their understanding, and their candor, will stand you in very good stead.

ACCEPTING THE OFFICE

As you accept the office of class leader, therefore, you will by no means be on your own. First, you will have the collegiality of other class leaders, with whom you will meet every month (below, p. 97). Then you will have the friendship and support of your weekly covenant discipleship group, who will be as concerned about your discipleship as about their own. Just as important, you will also have the affirmation of the congregation as a whole, because you will be publicly acknowlewdged at charge conference, and commissioned in public worship.

Along with this public affirmation, it is important that you also seek God's blessing on your decision in an extended time of prayer. Just as your call has come both inwardly and outwardly, so the confirmation must be inward and outward; and it is at this critical point that many of us trip up. We have wrestled with God's call, perhaps for a long time, and when finally we agree to answer it, we are so overwhelmed by the relief of reaching a decision that we forget to consult God at the very time we begin our new work.

This is a dangerous pitfall. We feel so assured by the outward confirmation of our decision, that we neglect to confirm it inwardly. We assume that our business with God was primarily the discerning of our call, and that once we have answered it, there is much less need to talk with God about it. However, "Don't call me, I'll call you," is no more wise an axiom once you have answered the call of Christ, than when you were first struggling to discern it. Whatever you do, don't make this mistake.

In fact, there is no time when we are in more urgent need of intensive prayer than immediately following an acceptance of God's call. This will most certainly be the case when you have accepted the invitation to become a class leader. It will be a time of great vulnerability, for you will have lowered your defenses in order to surrender to God's will. Just as this leaves you open to the grace of God, it also leaves you open to the forces of Beelzebul, the defeated ruler of this planet who refuses to leave the stage (Luke 11:14-23). And you can be sure Beelzebul will strike (Luke 11:24-26). Those of us who are servants of Jesus Christ in the world are not in neutral territory (Eph. 6:12).

PRAYERFUL PREPARATION

As soon as possible, find some extended time—a morning or afternoon, or a whole day if you can arrange it—during which you can reflect with God in prayer about your decision to become a class leader. You should try to do this away from your home and place of work, so that you can be completely focused in prayer. You may wish to follow a model for personal retreat. An excellent resource for this is *A Guide to Prayer for Ministers and Other Servants*, by Rueben P. Job and Norman Shawchuck, where there are guidelines for such a time, with suggested scriptural and devotional readings.[90] You may wish to make this retreat with other prospective class leaders; and if you do, you may also wish to invite the pastor to join you. Whether you do it alone or with others, however, the purpose of this time of prayer and reflection is for you personally to seek God's blessing on your decision. You have already been assured by the pastor and the congregation that you have done the right thing. But now you must be assured inwardly by the Holy Spirit. Much of your time as a class leader will be spent in forming other Christian disciples, and for this you will need to know who you are and what you are doing. Only the assurance of the Holy Spirit can equip you for such a task.

As you pray for this assurance, expect the attacks of Beelzebul. They will come as fresh doubts about your ability to do the work of a class leader, as discouragement and even despondency about the level of discipleship in your congregation, or as pessimism about whether anything can be done by anyone to form faithful disciples in such an unfaithful church. And if the attack is vigorous and sustained, you may even find yourself doubting your very discipleship.

Weather these attacks in the strength of Jesus Christ. Every time a doubt wells up within you, turn to one of the scriptures you have selected for your retreat—scriptures that focus on the call of God. For every uncharitable thought that crosses your mind about your fellow church members, think of persons who took time to form you in your discipleship, and how tolerant and forgiving they were of your shortcomings. For every obstacle you see in the task that lies ahead, turn to a passage from the saints of the church, and remember the words of the Methodist covenant prayer:

> I put myself wholly into your hands:
> put me to what you will, rank me with whom you will;
> put me to doing, put me to suffering,
> let me be employed for you, or laid aside for you,
> exalted for you, or trodden under foot for you;
> let me be full, let me be empty,
> let me have all things, let me have nothing,
> I freely and heartily resign all
> to your pleasure and disposal.[91]

You will come through this time of retreat, not only stronger in your calling, but also more practiced in quenching "the flaming arrows of the evil one" (Eph. 6:16). There could be no better preparation for your task of leading others in their walk with Christ.

THE LEADERS' MEETING

One of the first practical steps you will take as a class leader is to start attending the monthly leaders' meeting. This is described in more detail in the companion volume, *Forming Christian Disciples*, and is a priority for all class leaders and the pastoral staff of the congregation. It is in addition to, and quite distinct from, your weekly covenant discipleship group.

There are two purposes for the leaders' meeting, the first of which is to provide ongoing support and supervision for your work as a class leader. This is a setting in which you can feel free to share any aspect of your duties with the pastor and with the other leaders, and also where you can be regularly informed about the programs and activities available to church members. It will not be enough for you to present your class members with the General Rule of Discipleship. They will need specific information about how they can follow its guidelines in the world: how they can learn to witness to Jesus Christ, and how they can further their discipleship through acts of compassion, justice, worship, and devotion. The leaders' meeting provides a constant update on new resources, ideas, and learnings in these areas.

The second purpose of the leaders' meeting is to "take the pulse" of the congregation. Each month you will be asked to give a report on the discipleship of your class—not necessarily a progress report on each member, but an assessment of how your class as a whole is relating to the ministry and mission of the congregation. As you get to know your members, and discover their gifts and graces, you will gain a sense of where they need to develop their walk with Christ. By sharing these insights at the leaders' meeting, you will help the pastoral staff and the administrative council to plan church programs and ministries that are more fulfilling for the membership as a whole, and more beneficial to the community at large.

At the same time, you will be able to share some of the difficulties and frustrations of your class. Once again, this will not be a reporting of individual problems. You will be dealing with these in your regular contact with each member. Moreover, since your role is not to provide specialized pastoral care, as a matter of course you will be referring members to appropriate professional ministries of the church when they need them. The leaders' meeting is rather a means of identifying general problems and concerns among the congregation—quite ordinary needs that are often unmet, simply because they are unknown or unrecognized. Without breaking any confidentiality between you and your class members, the leaders' meeting thus makes it possible to determine where the care and concern of the congregation and the pastoral staff need to be focused.

CO-PASTOR OF THE CONGREGATION

One of the most important aspects of the leaders' meeting is its pastoral collegiality. You will find this developing, not only between yourself and the other class leaders, but also with the pastor—a new relationship for you both. To relate to your pastor as a colleague will require new understandings, and probably some major adjustments. But it is a collegiality that will be critical for the work you do with your class, and you should develop it as quickly and as positively as you can.

As a class leader, you are going to be in essence a co-pastor of the congregation. This does not mean that you will share in all the dimensions of pastoral leadership. The ministries of word and sacrament will remain with the ordained pastor, as will areas of professional competence, such as pastoral counseling. But rather than having pastoral duties delegated to you, you will now have your own area of responsibility. You will have pastoral oversight of a class of church members for the basics of their Christian living in the world. You will be their leader in discipleship, complementing and undergirding the pastoral ministry of the clergy, thus freeing your pastor for the work he or she has been ordained and trained to do.

YOUR ACCOUNTABILITY

You will, of course, be held accountable for what you do, and you will have supervision. To begin with, you will meet with your covenant discipleship group each week, in mutual accountability for your own walk with Christ. Then you will attend the monthly leaders' meeting, where you will be accountable to the other class leaders. You will also be accountable to the charge conference of the congregation, the body that first appoints you and then reappoints you each year.

The person to whom you are most immediately accountable, however, is the pastor. As the shepherd with ultimate responsibility for the flock, the pastor has been entrusted with the spiritual welfare of each member of the congregation. It is only appropriate, therefore, that your work as a co-pastor should remain under his or her supervision. If you develop the collegiality of a pastoral team, questions of authority and supervision will rarely be an issue. Much more, you will find that you strengthen and encourage each other's work—so much so that the flock for whom you share pastoral responsibility will increasingly look beyond itself into the world. The self-preoccupations of congregational life will become less and less important as you, the pastor, your fellow class leaders, and the members you are now pastoring, begin to reach out much more freely, intentionally, and effectively, in ministry and mission.

GETTING TO KNOW YOUR CONGREGATION

Your first task as a co-pastor is to get to know the congregation. This does not mean getting to know each individual member as much as it means getting to know the body as a whole—its characteristics as a community of faith, its relationship to the community at large, and its potential for ministry and mission as a sign of the coming reign of God. You will, of course, get to know the individual members of your class in more depth (see Chapter 6). But if you are to guide them in their discipleship, you need to have a sense of the community of faith in which their relationship with Christ is nurtured, and their walk with Christ is formed.

It is important, therefore, that you make every effort to find out what your congregation is doing to witness to Jesus Christ in the world, and to follow his teachings in light of the four-fold General Rule of Discipleship. Much of this information is probably known to you already, especially if you are a member of a covenant discipleship group, where your weekly accountability keeps you focused on the four areas of the Rule. As a class leader, however, you will be helping other people with their discipleship, and the range of their needs and interests will quickly convince you of the need to be well informed. As you acquaint yourself with what is happening in your congregation, you will be surprised at how much ministry is taking place, and how rich and varied it is. You will come to a much deeper appreciation of your church family.

GETTING TO KNOW YOUR WORLD

In addition to discovering how your congregation witnesses to Jesus Christ and follows his teachings, you will need to learn about the world in which you and your members live: the immediate world of your community, and the larger national and international world that is closer to us than ever before. The Christian disciple must not only be aware of planet earth, but must love it, reach out to it, and yearn for its salvation no less than Jesus Christ, who died for its salvation. As a class leader, you will need to know about the world in order to show your members how to be Christ-like in the world.

Even though belonging to a covenant discipleship group will give you an important start in this direction, you will still need to gather information about the world in which you live. Find the heartbeat of your community, and also its arteries. Become familiar with its places of strength and power, and also its places of weakness and vulnerability. Who are the people who most need affirmation, and who cannot take care of themselves? Where is ministry already taking place, and where is more help needed? What are the needs of the larger world, and how can ordinary people such as your class members play a part in meeting those needs?

As you ask these questions, keep in mind that the information you gather is for a purpose: to help your class members reach out in ministry and mission, so that they might witness to Jesus Christ and follow his teachings in the world he came to save. The question you are most likely to hear as you help to form their discipleship is, "What can *I* do?" Always be ready with an answer.

TRAINING "ON THE JOB"

Having discerned your call and prepared for your task as a class leader, you might be wondering about training. To assume this much responsibility in the life and work of the church would surely seem to require a time of qualification. Most especially would this seem to be the case with an office described as that of "co-pastor," considering how thorough is the training for pastors themselves.

The answer is that your training as a class leader will substantially take place "on the job." It is already clear from what we have said thus far that this does not mean a perfunctory approach to the task. Membership in a covenant discipleship group and appointment by charge conference are far from perfunctory, and the preparations we have just outlined require a marked degree of intentionality. Even so, for the most part you will learn how to perform your duties by doing them. You are not an authority on Christian living so much as a guide. You are not a counselor so much as a friend. You are not a paragon of discipleship so much as a fellow pilgrim. The difference is that you have accepted responsibility for leading others along the way; and you are able to do this quite simply because you have come to understand the importance of accountability in your discipleship.

As the number of congregations with class leaders increases, the General Board of Discipleship will sponsor weekend events designed to improve skills and develop resources. There will likewise be a growing network of class leaders through which information can be shared and new ideas fostered (see below, p. 161, n.111). As you come to know the needs and interests of your class members, your appetite will be whetted for the many and varied continuing education events constantly taking place throughout the church. The office of Covenant Discipleship and Christian Formation in Nashville will be pleased to provide such information on request.

FORMING YOUR CLASS

Allow your preparations to continue for as long as you feel the need. During this time you will be attending the leaders' meeting, and you will find the collegiality of your pastor and fellow class leaders helpful and reassuring. After several months, or whenever you feel ready, you should announce to the meeting that you wish to assume your duties, and to be assigned the fifteen to twenty church members who will comprise your class.

Do not worry about this—you do not have to pick and choose from the congregation! The entire process of assigning class members takes place in the leaders' meeting, with full and open discussion of all the factors that might affect the makeup of your class, such as where people live, age levels, special interests, or family groupings. You will, of course, have a full part in these discussions, for which the companion volume, *Forming Christian Disciples*, provides guidelines. But there is really only one firm rule: Each class is as representative as possible of the congregation as a whole. It defeats the purpose of your office if you are assigned "problem" members, or "inactives," or "target groups." If you sense that your class is being weighted in this way, register an immediate protest—though it is very unlikely this will happen. The discussions and assignments will be very collegial.

During this process you will have feelings of excitement and anticipation, as will the pastor and the other class leaders. In keeping with all its deliberations, the leaders' meeting will approach these assignments prayerfully, and the work of the Holy Spirit will become apparent as the decisions are made. When your class list is finalized, you will find yourself at the threshold of a tremendous new venture in your discipleship. You will feel humble, a little apprehensive, but more than ready to move ahead. You are now a class leader in the fullest sense: You have a class.

FOR REFLECTION

1. Do you experience the call of God as "a sense of unease, or restlessness, gradually leading to a conviction?" (p. 83)

2. In what ways do other people help you to discern a call from God?

3. Have you ever resisted a call from God on the grounds of false modesty? (p. 87)

4. "This table is open to those who love the Lord Jesus Christ, or would like to do so" (p. 89). Is this an appropriate invitation to the sacrament of Holy Communion?

5. How many people do you know who "do the best they can" for Jesus Christ? (p. 91)

6. What will it mean for you to "go professional" with your discipleship? (p. 91)

7. Do you have Christian friends with more gifts and graces than yourself? With less?

8. Is it a valid requirement that class leaders should belong to a covenant discipleship group?

9. How do you feel about spiritual retreats?

10. Has this chapter given you a better understanding of your pastor?

Chapter Six

Getting to Know Your Class

DIVERSITY OF PEOPLE

Getting to know the members of your class will be one of the most stimulating experiences of your life. It may also be one of the most unsettling, for the fact of the matter is that most of us are usually very selective about the people we get to know. We maintain a courteous and even cordial social contact with casual acquaintances, but we are very careful about those with whom we spend our time, and still more careful about those in whom we confide. The result is that we get to know very little about humanity in general until we are in the position of having to establish a relationship with people we don't know—or unless we happen to deal regularly with the public. It does not take long, working in a restaurant or a store, to become very seasoned about the wide range of people in the world. There is little about human nature that will surprise a taxi driver, a flight attendant, or a hospital orderly.

As you begin the process of getting to know your class members, you will discover how very different they are, and how quickly they can surprise you with their behavior and their attitudes. Even though they will have one important thing in common, namely, their membership in your congregation, they will present a much wider range of characteristics, temperaments, interests, habits, beliefs, and convictions, than you ever thought possible. This does not make them more or less different from other human beings, nor yet does it mean that you have led a sheltered or isolated life thus far. It simply means that you are now in the "people business." You are discovering what every pastor discovers in her or his first pastorate: that in creating the human race, God has made no two people alike. Human beings have infinite diversity. It will make your work as a class leader demanding at times, but also very exciting.

AN OPEN MIND

During these early contacts with your class members, it is important to keep an open mind, and to make no hasty judgments about
anything you see or hear. You may need to offer advice and as-
sistance in due course, and also some gentle correction—but not at
first, not during these introductory days and weeks as you and
your members get the measure of each other. You may be eager to
get to know them, but they are going to be cautious about you.
They will know that the whole point of your relationship with
them is to help them with their discipleship. And since this is the
most profound and meaningful aspect of their lives, their trust will
not be given lightly.

Their trust will be given much more readily, however, if they see
from the outset that you are not there to judge, but to help; that
you are not there to evaluate their discipleship, but to offer them
guidance in their walk with Christ; that you are not there to make
them feel inadequate, but rather to be a Christian companion along
the way. The openness with which you accept them as fellow
Christians will reassure them about their own discipleship—and
by the same token will affirm you in your own walk with Christ.
Meeting these new companions will reveal new and enriching
dimensions as you share your pilgrimage together.

DIVERSITY OF GIFTS AND GRACES

While the human diversity of your class members may well
surprise you, you will discover something else about them that
is deeply reassuring: a diversity of qualities that is undeniably
the work of God's grace in their lives. Each of your members will
have gifts and talents which, in addition to making them unique
human beings, give them tremendous potential for Christian discipleship.

As their class leader, it will be an important part of your task to
help your members identify these gifts and graces, and to use them
in service of Jesus Christ. But during this time of introduction, you
need not make this a topic of conversation unless they raise it first.
If you move too quickly into areas of personal concern, even areas
of affirmation, you may well make them apprehensive. Allow a
degree of mutual trust to develop before you engage in any kind of
self-assessment.

This will not prevent you, however, from noting the gifts and graces of your members. You will eventually find the right opportunity to introduce this aspect of their faith into your conversation; and in the meantime, you can focus on the basics of their discipleship—which is, of course, the whole point of your relationship with them.

You will find their gifts and graces falling into three general categories: (1) the qualities and talents that make each of them a unique human being; (2) the particular spiritual gifts that God has given each of them that make a unique contribution to the congregation; (3) the ways in which the Holy Spirit works in their lives so that the grace of God makes their discipleship more and more a reflection of the Christ they endeavor to honor and obey.

1. HUMAN QUALITIES AND TALENTS

One of the great weaknesses of congregational life today is that many of our members remain anonymous. Perhaps anonymous is too strong a word, in that members are usually (though by no means always) known by name. But far too many are known *only* by name, as if that alone establishes their identity and their place in the congregation. Indeed, the obsession with people's names at church events, especially at conferences or workshops, would be laughable if it were not so wearisome: large labels stuck to lapels, as often as not saying "Hello" before the person has had a chance to speak; or the premature (and sometimes presumptuous) use of first names, to establish a familiarity for which people are not always ready.

The reality is that most of us know very little about our fellow church members, even when we belong to a small membership church. One of your privileges as class leader, therefore, will be to know 15-20 of your fellow members in a meaningful way—a relationship that dispenses with nametags. It will be your privilege to know their human qualities: their intellectual abilities; their homespun wisdom; their physical talents; their emotional generosities; their patience, understanding, and sympathy; their ambition, determination, and vision; their willingness to help others; their concerns for social justice; their professional accomplishments; their recreational interests; their unusual hobbies. In short, getting to know these people will expose you to a greater richness of talent and human potential than you ever thought existed in your congregation.

2. SPIRITUAL GIFTS

The New Testament has many descripions of the spiritual gifts God bestows on those who are called to be Christian disciples. But none is more helpful than Paul's analogy of the Body of Christ:

> For as in one body we have many members, and not all the members have the same function, so we, who are many, are one body in Christ, and individually we are members one of another. We have gifts that differ according to the grace given to us: prophecy, in proportion to faith; ministry, in ministering; the teacher, in teaching; the exhorter, in exhortation; the giver, in generosity; the leader, in diligence; the compassionate, in cheerfulness (Rom. 12:4-8).

In another letter, the imagery is even more specific:

> Speaking the truth in love, we must grow up in every way into him who is the head, into Christ, from whom the whole body, joined and knit together by every ligament with which it is equipped, as each part is working properly, promotes the body's growth in building itself up in love (Eph. 4:15-16).

Each congregation of the church is a microcosm of this body of Christ; and in turn, your class will be a microcosm of the congregation. You can expect to find among your class members a range of spiritual gifts that truly reflect the congregation as a whole, and indeed the wider church. You may find a member who has the gift of *prophecy*—not necessarily in the technical sense of prophetic preaching or utterance, but in the ability to perceive and declare the will and the working of God in ways that the rest of us cannot see, or will not accept, until someone with this gift reveals it to us. Likewise there will be those with the gift of *ministry*, or *service*, who seek to help others primarily because God's Spirit gives them the motivation and the empathy to do so. This is not to say that the rest of us should sit back and give such persons the monopoly of service to others. On the contrary, they should be our role models.

With regard to the gifts of *teaching* and *exhortation*, the New Testament scholar, C. Kingsley Barrett, makes a helpful distinction. He suggests that both teaching and exhorting are a means of communication, but in different ways. Teachers communicate by way of explanation; exhorters communicate by way of application. The two go together in communicating the gospel, since the Christian message can "never be explained without application or applied without explanation."[92] You may find both of these gifts in your class: the person who can explain with great clarity, and the person who can show by example—precisely the gift that you will often bring to bear as a class leader.

You may have noticed that all of these spiritual gifts focus on "doing" rather than "being." This applies no less to the remaining spiritual gifts: *giving*, *leading*, and *compassion*. This is why the General Rule of Discipleship states that we will endeavor to follow the teachings of Jesus through *acts* of compassion, *acts* of justice, *acts* of worship, and *acts* of devotion; and this is why Paul instructs the Christians at Rome to *practice* their gifts of giving, leading, and compassion. Likewise, when you discern these gifts among your class members, you will sense a desire to practice charity, or a yearning to take the lead, or a concern to actually help the disadvantaged. Though once again, during this time of introduction between you and your class members, merely note these gifts where you find them. The opportunity to put them to use will come soon enough.

3. THE FRUIT OF THE SPIRIT

You are likely to find this third category of gifts and graces primarily among those members of your class who are seasoned in their discipleship. You will also find them more in the form of graces than of gifts, since they are developed through the work of the Holy Spirit in people's lives. The more a person walks with Christ, following his commandments in the world, the more the Holy Spirit is able to work in and through that person's life, producing what Paul calls the "fruit of the Spirit." We spoke of these qualities earlier in another context (above, p. 87), yet a reminder may be in order:

> The fruit of the Spirit is love, joy, peace, patience, kindness, generosity, faithfulness, gentleness, and self-control. There is no law against such things (Gal. 5:22-23).

The difference between "gifts" and "graces" is very clear once we consider this list. The spiritual gifts that Paul describes in Romans 12 are often found in persons who do not display the fruit of the Spirit; and by the same token, the fruit of the Spirit is often found in persons whose spiritual gifts are not at all self-evident. This means that obedience to Jesus Christ, following his teachings step by step and day by day, does not depend on the extent of our spiritual gifts, but rather on doing the best we can with the gifts we have been given. It is obedience to Christ that will open us to grace, which in turn will manifest itself in our lives through love, joy, peace, patience, kindness, generosity, faithfulness, gentleness, and self-control.

All of these gifts and graces—the human, the spiritual, and the fruit of the Spirit—you will find to a greater or lesser degree among your class members. Do not worry about recognizing all of them at once. You will not become an accomplished class leader over-night—nor should you be concerned about categorizing the gifts and graces of your members. The preceding lists are intended to give you an idea of the tremendous potential of your class rather than to furnish you with a diagnostic index. But the more you get to know your members, and the more you help them with their discipleship, the more informed you will become about their particular capacities for faithful service of Jesus Christ. Moreover, getting to know these spiritual dimensions of their lives will make you much more aware of your own.

DIVERSITY OF NEEDS

As you get to know the gifts and graces of your class members, you will also discover their needs. Indeed, there will probably be some of your members who are very quick to let you know what these are. The privatized culture in which we live has created many lonely people who have no one with whom they can talk; and even more important, no one they can trust. Once they realize that you are a trustworthy Christian friend, some of your class members may well seek to bend your ear at every opportunity.

While good listening is a worthwhile skill for you to develop in your work as a class leader, that is not the real purpose of your office. Without discouraging the openness that is essential to your relationship, it is important to make clear to your members that you are available primarily to assist them with their discipleship. If you sense any false expectations or misunderstandings about this role, emphasize that you are not a visitor on behalf of the church, and that you are certainly not a counselor. For one thing, your congregation probably has visitation, caring, and shepherd-ing ministries already in place—or should have. For another thing, you do not want to get into areas of pastoral care for which you are neither qualified nor have the time. Making all of this clear at the outset will make it much easier to focus on the basics of Christian discipleship as the foundation of your relationships.

Even so, do not be insensitive to your members' needs. These are likely to fall into two categories: dimensions of their lives where they need help; and dimensions where they need fulfill-ment. Put another way, some of your members are going to need help *from* other people; but some are going to need to give help *to* other people.[93] Surprisingly, it is this second category of need that you will most often find yourself called upon to address. There are many church members today who wish to exercise their discipleship in service to others, but who have never been chal-lenged to do so. You can be the means of providing them with the opportunity.

The place to deal with both of these needs is the monthly leaders' meeting. It may well be that other class leaders have similar needs among their members and can offer some suggestions. They may also have members in their classes who can provide specific as-sistance for the persons concerned.

By the same token, the monthly leaders' meeting gives you an opportunity to refer to the pastoral staff those problems that clearly require professional help. Of course, if you sense that the problem is urgent, you will wish to make that referral right away. Where possible, ask the person's permission to do so; but even if you do not feel able to ask permission, never hesitate to inform the pastor or an appropriate staff person in cases where you sense an urgent need. The pastoral staff of your congregation are trained to make inquiries and offer the help that is needed; and your promptness in making the referral may well make all the difference in the effec-tiveness of the help a person receives.

We shall deal in Chapter 7 with the more routine needs of your members, both in terms of being helped and of helping others. But during these introductory days and weeks, the ground rule is to take your questions and concerns to the leaders' meeting. You do not have to break confidentiality. You can talk generally about "my class," or "a member of my class," and you will quickly find that other class leaders are encountering many of the same needs among their members. Moreover, the pastoral staff of the congrega-tion will always be at these monthly meetings, to offer appropriate advice or intervention.

DIVERSITY OF FAITH

Another diversity among your class members will be their faith, and this too may surprise you. Let it quickly be said that diversity of faith does not mean diversity of religion. You may well find that some of your members have questions about other religions, and you may wish to become more informed in this regard as a point of mutual interest. Diversity of faith rather means that people have different kinds of faith, and faith in many different things. Moreover, during the course of a lifetime, their faith goes through changes of perception and commitment, a process known as faith development.

One of the foremost scholars in this field is James W. Fowler, who has been lecturing and writing on the subject for many years. You may wish to become better acquainted with his work, and there is no better place to start than with his most recent book, *Weaving the New Creation*. In order to understand faith development, Fowler explains, we must distinguish between faith, religion, and belief.[94] While this may sound like splitting hairs, in fact it helps us to understand the diversity of faith we find in the world. It also helps to explain the wide range of commitment we find in the average congregation, and that you are likely to find in your class.

1. FAITH AS A HUMAN UNIVERSAL

First of all, we must accept that faith is a human universal. Everyone has the potential for faith, and most people have faith in something. In this universal sense of the word, says Fowler, faith is "a dynamic pattern of personal trust and loyalty," by which we "rest our hearts [and] focus our life in persons, causes, ideals, or institutions that have great worth to us." People place this kind of faith in "images and realities of power," in "basic values," and in "shared stories."[95]

For example, millions of Americans have faith in the United States of America (a reality of power), and every Fourth of July they affirm the American way of life (a basic set of values) made possible by the American Revolution (a shared story). Yet on the same Fourth of July, there is also a marked diversity of faith. Native Americans have a very different view of the power of the United States and its basic values. Moreover, they share a very different story—as do African Americans, for whom it is difficult even now to have faith in a Declaration of Independence that has hardly made them equal in the eyes of many of their fellow citizens.

In other words, faith is not something uniquely Christian. It is a human characteristic that can be focused on any number of "persons, causes, ideals, or institutions," and it may surprise you to find how diverse, and how numerous, the faiths of your class members prove to be.

2. RELIGIOUS FAITH

To understand faith as a human universal further helps us to see that religion is a particular expression of faith. As Fowler explains it, religious faith is to place one's trust in traditions and beliefs that have been shaped across hundreds and thousands of years by the commitments of countless human beings.[96] These traditions are expressed in many ways: in oral teachings, in sacred writings, in art, and in music. But whatever the form, religious faith is ultimately a means of relating people to God. It is faith in a relationship that transcends human understanding.

Once again, religious faith is not unique to Christianity. As we have already noted, there are many world religions offering and advocating ways to know God. By the same token, there are some questionable forms of religious faith that focus on worldly values in the name of God. For the Christian, however, religious faith means placing ultimate trust in Jesus of Nazareth, the Christ whom God raised from the dead. Christ, and Christ alone, is the way to God, and Christian discipleship is the only way for the Christian to live.

3. RELIGIOUS BELIEFS

A further distinction Fowler helps us make in our understanding of faith development is that religious faith and religious beliefs are not the same thing. Religious faith is expressed and communicated through religious beliefs, but faith is much more profound than beliefs. Our faith is what we *do* with what we believe. Thus, to believe in Jesus Christ is not the same as having faith in Jesus Christ. I may believe that Jesus Christ is the Son of God. But only when I put my trust in him, make him the center of all my values, and seek to obey his teachings in my daily living in the world, can I be said to have faith in him. As we noted in Chapter 2, true faith in Jesus Christ leads to maturity of discipleship, and true discipleship deepens our faith in Jesus Christ.

One of the ways you will be able to help your class members is by showing them how their Christian beliefs are not the same as their Christian faith. Their beliefs are of course very important, because they are the means of expressing and communicating their faith: belief in the person of Jesus Christ, God the human being; the story of his life, death, and resurrection; the good news of the salvation he has accomplished for us; and the announcement of the reign of God that is coming, on earth as in heaven, through the ongoing work of the Holy Spirit. To hold these Christian beliefs, however, is not the same as having Christian faith. Disciples must take the further step of living in the world according to these beliefs—of giving such trusting obedience to the risen Christ, that their lives impart the grace and the power of the gospel in which they believe. In other words, the faith of Christian disciples must be the embodiment of their beliefs.

STAGES OF FAITH

Since faith is not merely a set of beliefs, but a way of life, it stands to reason that faith is dynamic, not static. The aspect of Fowler's work for which he is best known is his formulation of "stages" of faith through which people may pass during their lifetime. With respect to faith as a human universal, there are, according to Fowler, seven "positions," or "stages of faith consciousness," involving us in a "process of maturation and growth as we move from one season of our life to the next." These positions begin with infancy, and move through childhood and adolescence to adulthood and maturity. Each stage has its own integrity, which means that a person's faith may or may not develop at the same pace as physical and psychological growth. But in general, we can expect persons at differing stages of life to be at differing stages of faith. Their trust and their loyalty will be lived out in different ways, and their beliefs will likewise be expressed differently during their lifetime.[97]

When a person's faith becomes Christian faith, something else happens. The grace of God impacts a person's natural faith capacity with a spiritual dimension that is nothing short of a regeneration. There is "a more dramatic and radical process of recentering in our lives, a process of conversion, a *metanoia*, leading to the transformation and intensification of faith." There is a "dance of faith development . . . that has these twin movements: of maturation

and development, on the one hand, and of recentering and transformation in Christ, on the other." Indeed, so powerful is this
gracious transformation, that Christians must constantly take stock
of their natural faith development, lest they find themselves with a
faith stance and set of beliefs that are "out of date" in relation to the
impact God's grace is having on their lives.[98]

This is not the place to explore faith development in any further
detail. At some point you will wish to consult Fowler's work, and
that of other scholars in this field.[99] Their concepts will impress
upon you that everyone has a capacity for faith which develops
throughout life, and that Christian discipleship is a powerful, and
sometimes dramatic, transformation of this faith into a life that is
Christ-centered. Your task as a class leader will be to help your
members with the basics of their discipleship, at whatever stage of
faith they happen to be, and whatever point in this transformation
they happen to have reached. The Holy Spirit is of course the
transforming agent in their lives; but you can help them to be open
to the Spirit's grace and power.

"DEGREES OF FAITH"

It so happens that acknowledging the development of faith has
been a mark of Methodism from its earliest years. Chapter 2 of the
companion volume, *Covenant Discipleship*, describes how John
Wesley took a firm stand on this issue at the beginning of his
ministry. In 1740, at the Fetter Lane Society in London, some
members had taken the position that faith was a once-for-all
change in a person's life. According to this view, you either had a
"full assurance" of faith, or you did not have faith at all. There was
no in-between. In fact, the people who took this position went so
far as to insist that those who did not have "fullness of faith"
should cease from all other Christian activities until they received it
as a divine blessing. They were instructed to wait for this gift
passively and quietly—thus the name "Quietist"—because any
other kind of faith was not saving faith. By contrast, Wesley declared that there were "degrees of faith," since the scriptures
plainly showed that persons with weak faith still had a valid
faith.[100]

Today, there are still those who argue that you either "have
faith" or you "don't have faith." But in the Methodist tradition,
we follow Wesley's lead in affirming "degrees of faith." We also

follow his teaching that there is growth in discipleship. Faithful Christians become more surefooted in their walk with Christ as they become more seasoned in their obedience to his teachings in the world.

THE CHRISTIAN LIFE

When all is said and done, however, the simplest and most powerful imagery for Christian transformation is in the Bible—the analogy of life itself. The New Testament speaks eloquently of the new life we have in Christ Jesus (2 Cor. 5:17, Gal. 6:15, Eph. 4:24, Col. 3:10). Just as we are conceived, born, and grow through childhood to maturity, physically, mentally, and emotionally, so we are born into new life in the power of the Holy Spirit, and grow to the maturity of seasoned Christian discipleship (Eph. 4:13).

1. THE NEW BIRTH

The first stage in the new life with Christ is the new birth. Drawn from the gospel and the epistles of John (Jn. 3:3-8; 1 Jn. 3:9, 4:7, 5:18), it was the cutting edge of Methodist evangelistic preaching. John Wesley published a number of sermons on the subject, and in society meetings, classes, and bands, it was regarded as the foundational experience of Christian discipleship.[101]

It happens to be a good image. It is very human, and it allows for a wide range of experience. Think of it. No two births are alike, as any mother will readily verify. Some are quick and easy; others are long and labored. Just as important, the birth itself is not an isolated event. It is preceded by conception (a moment that is God's secret, not even revealed to the parents), and then by growth in the womb. Step by step the new life is formed, until it is ready to emerge into the world.

There is another interesting aspect to the image. In physical life, while the transition from womb to world is indeed a radical one, the form of the baby is not radically changed. As any parent will again testify, the first appearance of a child is not very flattering. It takes several days before references to family likeness are genuinely appreciated. The fact of the matter is that a baby is as formed the day before it is born as the day after. The change is rather one of dependence to independence. Before birth, the baby is entirely dependent on the mother for its life. Whereas after birth, while still heavily dependent, the baby is now breathing, feeding and growing with a marked new degree of *in*dependence. It is now a human being in its own right.

So it is with the Christian life. Our spiritual origins are God's secret. The precise moment when grace begins to work in our lives cannot be discerned, either by us, or by those who foster our spiritual welfare. But the signs of grace quickly begin to appear: a hunger for God's love and guidance; a yearning for God's justice and order in the world; and a growing dissatisfaction with the way things are, in our own lives and in the world. All of this brings us to a critical turning point, as conviction of our own sin, and the abhorrence of the sin which surrounds us, finally become unbearable. It is then that we surrender to God's grace, and are "born of the Spirit."

One of the great confusions in the church today is the stereotyping of this new birth as a particular kind of "conversion" experience. In some ways, this is understandable, since the decision to accept the forgiveness and reconciliation that God offers us in Jesus of Nazareth is indeed a critical repentance—a turning toward God that is a true *conversion*.[102] For most of us, however, this conversion does not happen dramatically, as it did with Saul on the Damascus road (Acts 9:1-9). It happens more gradually, especially for those of us who are born into Christian families and grow up in Christian congregations. Step by step, we come to realize the predicament of our sin and the bankruptcy of our self-sufficiency. And the critical turning point, when we finally come to know the joy and the peace of God's forgiveness and reconciliation, may happen in ways that are difficult to pinpoint.

The confusion lies in assuming that the new birth, or conversion, has to follow a prescribed pattern and experience; whereas each of us comes to know Jesus Christ, and returns to the family of God, in a unique way. No two "new births" are alike. Since the stereotyping of this is widespread in the church, however, you may have members in your class who do not regard themselves as true Christian disciples, or even as true Christians, because they have not experienced the "right kind" of new birth. The best way to clear this confusion is to ask any such person the obvious question: "Do you believe in Jesus Christ *now*, and do you want to be his disciple *now*?" If the answer is yes, then that person *is* born again, and ready to be formed as a Christian disciple.

It matters not at all whether he or she can recall being converted. After all, who can remember their first birth?

2. GROWTH IN CHRIST

Those who have anything to do with the birthing of new life will know that, while infants are very vulnerable, they also begin life with a tremendous energy and with awesome reserves of strength. The vigor with which infants will make their presence known, or the determination with which they will demand their food, are vivid memories for anyone who has been subjected to their demands. This was strikingly demonstrated in the 1985 earthquake in Mexico City, when a very young baby was discovered in the rubble after nine days. The baby was still alive, though the parents had long since died.

So it is with the new life in Christ. The new birth brings a vigor and a spiritual strength that surprises everyone, not least those who have helped in the birthing of this new follower of Christ. The strength and vigor of a new disciple can leave us all breathless. Yet just as important is the fact that this burst of energy cannot be sustained, and most certainly cannot be self-sustained. For not only does the new birth *imply* growth, it *requires* growth. It *demands* it. Babies will live and grow, or they will die. They cannot live and remain the way they are. However much parents might wish to keep their children as lovable, cuddlesome babies, they will inevitably change.

Of course, all parents wish to see their children alive and healthy. This is why parents give infants the food, the warmth, and the nourishment that will enable them to grow. Just as the mother once gave all of this through her womb, so now the parents continue to provide it through the family. Food is important, but it is not enough; warmth is important, but not enough; freedom of movement is important, but not enough; love is important, but even that is not enough. All of these provisions are necessary, and they must also be kept in balance.

The same applies to the life of the Christian disciple. The church nurtures the new life of a new Christian in its womb, until she or he is ready to accept the new life in Christ for her or himself. But then must follow the nourishment that will lead to healthy life and sustained growth. And just as the provisions for physical and emotional well-being must be kept in balance, so the necessities of the Christian life must be kept in balance for the new disciple if there is to be healthy spiritual growth.

We have already referred to the General Rule of Discipleship as the basic "diet" for this growth:

> To witness to Jesus Christ in the world,
> and to follow his teachings
> through acts of compassion, worship, and devotion,
> under the guidance of the Holy Spirit.

The importance of the rule is that it gives equal emphasis to all of the disciplines of the Christian life, directing the disciple toward the teachings of Jesus with equal emphasis. The sooner Christians accept the need for this balanced approach to discipleship, the more quickly and surely they will grow in obedience to Christ, and become seasoned disciples.

3. MATURITY IN CHRIST

One of the most valuable insights of John Wesley's theology is that growth in Christian discipleship is a constantly transforming work of grace. By establishing at the outset of his ministry that faith is not an "either/or," but a gift that comes in greater measure as faithful disciples obey the commandments of Jesus Christ in the world, Wesley taught Methodists to expect a maturity in their discipleship. They did not regard grace as ineffectual in their lives. They expected to be changed.[103]

Unfortunately, this Methodist teaching on Christian maturity has been allowed to lapse. Clergy and laity alike today are not sure what it means, due in no small measure to the name by which it has most commonly been known, the doctrine of "Christian perfection." People are uncomfortable with the notion that some Christians might be more advanced than others. Yet it stands to reason that if there is growth in the Christian life, there must also be maturity—and likewise, immaturity. These distinctions do not mean a difference in the love God bestows on Christians, nor do they mean a greater status in the family of God for some as opposed to others. But if Christian discipleship is a life of discipline, as the word implies, then those who practice the discipline more regularly and more faithfully are going to become more mature as Christians; and that's that.

A family anecdote may help to illustrate the point. When our daughter was five years old, she decided one morning to give my wife and myself breakfast in bed. She really put her heart and soul into it—a full, cooked breakfast. What a wonderful gesture! Unfortunately, not to put too fine a point on it, the meal was a disaster. To begin with, she brought it to us at 5:00 A.M. The eggs were barely formed; the bacon was limp, with puddles of grease; the coffee was lukewarm, with things floating in it; and the toast was a burnt offering. Desperately trying to focus our wits at such an early hour, my wife and I had a brainwave. We observed that we had no sugar for the coffee, and asked our daughter if she would mind getting it for us. While she was gone, we quickly scooped the food on to some tissues in the bathroom, so that when she returned we were able to display empty plates, and say what a wonderful meal it had been. The beam on her face as she sat at the end of the bed will remain a lifetime memory. Needless to say, had she done the same thing at age ten, or fifteen, we would not have been so charitable. But at age five, all the imperfections of the meal were nothing compared to the love she showed us, and the pleasure she received from doing it.

So it is with Christian discipleship. Our early efforts are often clumsy, ill-timed, and lacking in accomplishment. When our motive is to serve Jesus Christ, these childlike imperfections are overlooked. But if we have grown in years of Christian discipleship, and have not advanced beyond these early efforts, they become childish and infantile—because our desire to serve Jesus Christ has clearly weakened. Indeed, this is why so many Christians lose their way. They do not practice obedience to Christ; and then they wonder why their relationship with Christ is not as warm and assuring as it used to be.

Those of us with responsibility for leadership in the church must do everything we can to make sure this does not happen. We must encourage and coach our members in practicing the General Rule of Discipleship, so that their lives are formed by the teachings of Jesus, and constantly filled with the grace of the Holy Spirit. In this way, not only will their discipleship develop according to the teachings of Jesus, as they apply themselves to acts of compassion, justice, worship, and devotion; but also their relationship with Christ will deepen, as the presence of the Holy Spirit in their lives opens them to the very mind of God.

CONSTANCY OF GRACE

Therein lies the true dynamic of Christian discipleship: the constancy of grace. This is not to say that grace is uniform. On the contrary, God's grace is as diverse as discipleship itself. But grace is constant: it is present in the life of every human being, and it is the moving force in our salvation, inviting, encouraging, challenging, directing, empowering, and ultimately enfolding us with the love of God. Moreover, it is present at each stage of the new life we have in Christ Jesus, nudging us forward to an ever-deepening relationship with God, and transforming us into ever more faithful disciples.

There are many places in the writings of John Wesley where this is well explained. But there is no better example than the following passage from his sermon, "On Working Out Our Own Salvation:"

Salvation begins with what is usually termed (and very properly) "preventing grace"; including the first wish to please God, the first dawn of light concerning his will, and the first slight, transient conviction of having sinned against him. All these imply some tendency toward life, some degree of salvation, the beginning of a deliverance from a blind, unfeeling heart, quite insensible of God and the things of God. Salvation is carried on by "convincing grace," usually in scripture termed "repentance," which brings a larger measure of self-knowledge, and a farther deliverance from the heart of stone. Afterwards we experience the proper Christian salvation, whereby "through grace" we "are saved by faith," consisting of those two grand branches, justification and sanctification. By justification we are saved from the guilt of sin and restored to the favor of God: by sanctification we are saved from the power and root of sin, and restored to the image of God. All experience, as well as Scripture, shows this salvation to be both instantaneous and gradual. It begins the moment we are justified, in the holy, humble, gentle, patient love of God and man. It gradually increases from that moment, as a "grain of mustard seed, which at first is the least of all seeds, but" gradually "puts forth large branches," and becomes a great tree; till in another instant the heart is cleansed from all sin, and filled with pure love to God and man. But even that love increases more and more, till we "grow up in all things into him that is our head," "till we attain the measure of the stature of the fullness of Christ."[104]

DIVERSITY OF DISCIPLESHIP

By now, you may be wondering why we have gone to such lengths to identify stages of growth in Christian discipleship, to say nothing of the distinctions between faith, Christian faith, and Christian beliefs. If the task of a class leader is to help people with the basics of their discipleship, why the need for all this information? Does it not conflict with the opening chapter of the book, in which it was stressed that class leaders are appointed primarily to show people the ropes and to lead by example?

This is a point well taken. So let it quickly be said that the purpose of this information is first of all to prepare you for the wide diversity of discipleship you may find among the members of your class. Not only are they likely to be at different places in their path to Christian maturity. You may also find them at different stages in how they live out their faith. Indeed, their faith may not be exclusively focused on Jesus Christ. They may have other faiths, mingling or even conflicting with their commitment to Jesus Christ.

A good example of a conflicting faith is nationalism, which in the United States of America is often identified with faith in God, if not in Jesus Christ. The symbols are powerfully present in most church sanctuaries—the stars and stripes on prominent display alongside Christian insignia. This is not to say that nationalism is an undesirable quality in a Christian disciple. But it is to say that whenever loyalty and love for one's country conflict with loyalty and love for Jesus Christ, there can be no question which faith is the more important. You may also find some diversity in the beliefs through which your class members express their faith— beliefs that you find difficult to reconcile with your own understanding of Christian discipleship. For example, some people have a view of the Bible which others regard as too narrow, or too liberal; others have differing beliefs with regard to the ethical issues debated in the church. But you can be sure of one thing: Whatever the faith of your members, whatever their religious beliefs, and whatever the maturity of their Christian discipleship, grace will be at work in their lives. Your task, therefore, is to focus their faith on their discipleship, so that grace may work even more abundantly. It will then be your privileged delight to see them "grow in the grace and knowledge of our Lord and Savior Jesus Christ" (2 Peter 3:18).

GROWTH IN DISCIPLESHIP

As the relationship deepens between you and your class, and as mutual trust increases, the principles of faith development and growth in discipleship will further stand you in good stead as you begin to discern the transformation in their lives, and yours, brought about by the Holy Spirit. For you will observe something else about Christian discipleship that is similar to life in general: Growth is not always steady, nor is it irreversible. As with life in general, so in the Christian life, even the most mature can stumble. Indeed, it is a mark of maturity to know that there *will* be lapses into immaturity. Of course, these are not acceptable as a permanent state of affairs; but the mature person is aware that they will happen. The most sophisticated man can become a sulky little boy when his football team loses. The most sensitive woman can become a spoiled little girl in heavy traffic.

In the same way, even the most seasoned Christian disciple can slip into immaturity, rebelling against God, and reverting to childish attitudes and habits. In the long run, our growth in grace will make us consistent in our obedience. But we must never assume that we are immune from disobedience. We can always stumble. By the same token, just as little children can often be wise beyond their years, so those who are just starting out as Christian disciples often have a great deal to teach the rest of us, not least because of their unembarrassed eagerness to love and serve Jesus Christ. Not without good reason did Jesus make a little child the model for entering the kingdom of heaven (Matt. 18:1-5).

CHRIST-CENTERED DISCIPLESHIP

All of these diversities—of faith in general, of religious beliefs, of faith in Jesus Christ, of growth in grace, and of maturity in discipleship—all of these variables make it vitally important that you focus your class members on obedience to Jesus Christ. Whatever their stage of commitment, whatever their Christian beliefs, whatever the level of their spiritual maturity, they can all follow the basic teachings of Jesus. This is why the General Rule of Discipleship consists of such practical guidelines—what we *do* for Jesus Christ, irrespective of our faith, our maturity, or our immediate feelings. The guiding principle of Christian discipleship should, indeed must, always be Christ-centeredness in all things at all times.

Without this anchor, Christian disciples are at the mercy of stormy seas.

We looked at these stormy seas in Chapter 4, and they are addressed at some length in Chapter 3 of the companion volume, *Forming Christian Disciples*. But they are worth emphasizing one more time as you prepare to assume your duties as a class leader. One of the great challenges of being a Christian in late twentieth century North America is the consuming self-centeredness of our culture. People are conditioned by all sorts of social pressures to make their own welfare an absolute priority, and to seek self-fulfillment and self-gratification as their end in life. To a degree that is not always recognized, still less acknowledged, the church has succumbed to these pressures, and as a result Christian discipleship is often viewed merely as another means of self-fulfillment. In congregational life today, the benefits of being a Christian are featured far more often than the obligations.

The only way to meet this challenge is to center every dimension of our discipleship on Jesus Christ—not the Christ we often use as a rubber stamp for what we have already decided, but the Christ who was Jesus of Nazareth, a human being who lived a very particular lifestyle, and who left us with some very particular commandments to follow. This is why the General Rule of Discipleship focuses on Jesus Christ at every point: To witness to *Jesus Christ* in the world, and to follow the teachings of *Jesus Christ* through acts of compassion, justice, worship, and devotion, thereby providing a Christ-centered form of discipleship that can be empowered by the guidance of the Holy Spirit.

If you help your members to center their lives on Jesus Christ, then the diversity of their discipleship can be limitless. For with Christ at the center, each member is free to be as different as the gifts and graces God bestows. But if Christ is not at the center, then however diverse your class may appear to be, in fact they will have a tedious sameness. They will shape their discipleship according to their own ideas, their own strengths, and their own preferences. Not only will this seriously weaken their relationship with Christ. It will also prove to be singularly lacking in imagination. For there is nothing more boring than Christian disciples pleasing themselves—as the world is always quick to recognize.

A WORD OF ENCOURAGEMENT

The preceding pages may have overwhelmed you, or at least left you feeling very unprepared to begin your task. It is important therefore to remember that this is a handbook to be used many times as you carry out your duties. If there are parts you do not understand, discuss them with your fellow class leaders, or with your pastor. Use the reflection questions at the end of each chapter, and raise some of them at the leaders' meeting.

Above all, regard this book merely as the first of your resources as a class leader. You are now a co-pastor of the congregation, and the most effective training you receive will be on the job. Moreover, you are already well prepared. You are a disciple of Jesus Christ, holding yourself accountable week by week for your own obedience to Christ. This makes you very ready to meet your class members. You will gain knowledge and experience as you proceed.

FOR REFLECTION

1. Are you usually careful about those with whom you spend your time, and even more careful about those in whom you confide? (p. 105)

2. Have you ever looked for God's gifts and graces in other people's lives? In your own?

3. Is your congregation "a microcosm of the Body of Christ"? (p. 108)

4. Can you think of persons in your congregation who need help from other people? Who need to help others?

5. Can you think of other examples of faith that people have in "images and realities of power, in basic values, and in shared stories"? (p. 112)

6. Do you have Christian beliefs that differ from those of other members of your congregation? Do these differences prevent you from working together as Christian disciples?

7. What can you recall of your new birth in Christ?

8. Do you feel that you are maturing as a Christian disciple? Can you think of times when you have lapsed into immaturity? (pp. 119, 123)

9. What are the social and cultural pressures that make it difficult for you to be a faithful disciple?

10. Do you agree that discipleship not centered on Jesus Christ has a "tedious sameness"? (p. 124)

Chapter Seven

Forming the Discipleship Of Your Class

ESTABLISHING CONTACT WITH YOUR MEMBERS

Once your class has been assigned by the leaders' meeting (above, p. 101), it is important to establish contact with your members as soon as you can, to invite them to be in your class. Do this first of all by personal letter, letting them know how pleased you are to have this opportunity of working with them as a Christian colleague. Point out in the letter that you are available primarily to help them with their discipleship, and to be a source of information about the life and work of the congregation. Let them know that they can expect you to visit them personally in the near future, when you will explain the nature and purpose of your office more fully, and ask them to confirm that they wish to be in your class.

As you schedule these visits, or perhaps while you are making them, there may be people on the list who do not wish to be in your class. Since the names were agreed by the leaders' meeting, including the pastor, this is not likely to happen very often. But when it does, you may be disappointed, and perhaps a little hurt. Report any such refusals to the leaders' meeting, and ask for the reaction of your colleagues. You will probably find that every class leader has had similar refusals; in these early days of recovering the office of class leader, this is bound to happen. The important thing is that no one should feel pressured into accepting your leadership. The idea will take time to grow in each congregation. But it will gain acceptance, as will you and your fellow class leaders. The person who refuses to join your class this year may well ask to join next year.

THE FIRST VISIT TO YOUR MEMBERS

The first visit to your members is extremely important. You will of course have occasion for informal contacts with some of your members during normal church activities, but casual meetings such as these are not a substitute for a visit to each member's home. Moreover, there are bound to be some of your class whom you do not meet regularly at church.

The tone you set for this visit should be cordial, but it should have a clear agenda. This can be helped by indicating in advance that it will last no more than 45-50 minutes, and that you need to talk only with your class member. If an entire family has been assigned to your class, then you will want to schedule a time when everyone can be present. But it may be that only one person in a family is in your class, and you will then need to make sure that you are not interrupted. By the same token, you will want to ensure that the distractions of home life today are not allowed to interfere, television being the most pervasive and the most troublesome. If necessary, ask to talk in another room. It may be difficult for you to act firmly in this way, but the sooner your members realize that you and they have the business of discipleship to transact, the stronger will be the foundation of your relationship with them.

THE AGENDA OF THE VISIT

By limiting the time of your visit to fifty minutes, you not only establish clear parameters for your conversation; you also establish a considerable freedom within those limits. It is one of the great fallacies of personal conversation that it must always be unstructured, to allow for people to get to know each other at their own pace. In fact, this can often waste a great deal of time. Unstructured conversation is fine for those who know each other well, and can enjoy each other's company. But for persons who are not well acquainted, knowing that a conversation has clear limits can often make it much more focused, and thus free from the pressure of wondering how and when to get to the business in hand. John Wesley understood this very well, and to this day candidates seeking ordination as elders of The United Methodist Church are publicly asked whether they will observe Wesley's directive to "visit from house to house" yet never to "spend any more time at any one place than is strictly necessary."[105]

Four items should be on the agenda during your visit. It will be helpful to share these with your class member at the beginning of the conversation, and at the same time let him or her know that there will be time for questions before you leave.

1. EXPLAIN THE OFFICE OF CLASS LEADER

If all the procedures for introducing class leaders into the congregation have been followed (see Part 3 of the companion volume, *Forming Christian Disciples*), the members of your class will know something of the nature and purpose of the office. It is unlikely, however, that they will have a clear picture of what is involved, and it will be helpful for them to hear this from you directly.

Before you make these visits, therefore, prepare a short description of the office of class leader, and how it relates to the life and work of the congregation as a whole. Rehearse this statement, not to the point where it becomes a recitation, but where you know what you want to say, and how to say it. You may find the *Christian Formation Brochure* helpful in this regard (order no. M299L), and you might also draw on some of the imagery we used in Chapter 4 (above, pp. 75-77). The clearer you are about your responsibilities, the more accepting your members will be of your leadership. After you have shared your statement, invite questions, and ascertain that they do in fact wish to belong to your class. If they wish to take some time over their decision, there is no need to remove them from your class list. You can keep in touch periodically until they know what they wish to do.

2. PERSONAL INTRODUCTIONS

It may seem out of place to have this second on the agenda, but there is a very good reason for explaining the nature and purpose of your office before introducing yourself more fully. We are not talking here about the preliminary courtesies that you will obviously exchange on the doorstep, but the personal information two people share when they are in the process of getting acquainted: family background, place of work, congregational activities, etc. The reason for holding this as the second item on the agenda is that any apprehension your class members might have about your role as a class leader can thus be eased at the very beginning. Once you have declared who you are and why you are there, conversation will be much more relaxed, and the remainder of the visit much more productive.

Knowing how you perceive yourself as a class leader will also help your members to accept you first and foremost as a Christian colleague, and not as an authority figure. While you have something to offer them by way of guidance and experience, you are essentially a companion in the walk with Christ; and with this clearly established, personal introductions can be a further means of laying the foundations of your relationship.

3. THE GENERAL RULE OF DISCIPLESHIP

The next item on the agenda should be the General Rule of Discipleship. Since this will be the substance of your conversation, you might find it helpful to copy the following diagram to leave behind at the end of your visit.

THE GENERAL RULE OF DISCIPLESHIP

To witness to Jesus Christ in the world, and to follow his teachings through acts of compassion, justice, worship, and devotion, under the guidance of the Holy Spirit.

[WORKS OF MERCY]

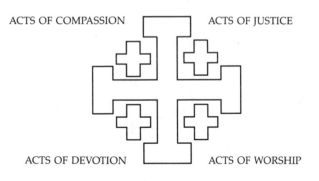

ACTS OF COMPASSION   ACTS OF JUSTICE

ACTS OF DEVOTION   ACTS OF WORSHIP

[WORKS OF PIETY]

As you describe the General Rule, it will be important to make clear that it is not designed to impose a rigid set of regulations, but rather to provide a shape, or form, for Christian discipleship. This is why it is called a "general" rule—something that everyone can attempt to follow at whatever stage in their Christian pilgrimage they happen to be. You will wish to make clear, however, that witnessing to Jesus Christ, and following his teachings through acts of compassion, justice, worship, and devotion, are basic obligations of Christian discipleship that the Holy Spirit calls on all Christians to fulfill to the best of their ability. Impress on your members that you are not asking them to become exemplary Christian disciples. But as their class leader, you are going to ask them to do *something* in each of the areas of the General Rule, so that their lives can increasingly be shaped by grace through obedience to Jesus Christ.

4. RESPONSE AND DISCUSSION

Leave ten or fifteen minutes at the end of the visit for the member to respond to what you have said, and to discuss any questions he or she might have. Some of your members may already be active in the congregation, and this will be an opportunity for you to provide affirmation and encouragement. You can explain how their activities relate to the General Rule, and show how they are already fulfilling some of its guidelines. On the other hand, some of your class members will probably find the General Rule a new concept. They may find it illuminating, and a means of opening new possibilities for their discipleship; or they may find it threatening, and wonder whether it is a form of legalism.

This is where your participation in a covenant discipleship group gives you a head start. Not only will such resistance be familiar to you (indeed, you probably voiced the same objections yourself when you joined your group). You will also be ready with some answers that are equally familiar to you from your covenant discipleship meetings. In other words, you do not need to worry what to say to your class members. You are one step ahead of them by virtue of your weekly accountability. You know the territory.

THIS IS JUST THE BEGINNING

Start to bring the visit to a close after 45 minutes, so that you can conclude promptly. Use these closing minutes to let the member know that you will be back in touch in a month or so to ask in which area of the General Rule she or he would first like your help. This will give time for further reflection on your visit, and also on the General Rule of Discipleship. Perhaps this is the first time that anyone from the congregation has presented this member with Christian obligations in such a clearcut way. In addition to the diagram of the General Rule, therefore, plan to leave a copy of the *Christian Formation Brochure*, which not only explains the office of class leader, but also has details of further resources.

As we noted in Chapter 6, discipleship has become largely a matter of personal preference in the church of today, and the idea that Jesus Christ requires our obedient service as a condition of being his disciple may ring strange in a number of ears. It may also cause some discomfort, so you will need to assure your members that, even though you do not plan to be in touch for another month, they should feel free to approach you with any questions they might have. Allow them to work through their encounter with the General Rule, but do not abandon them.

Before you leave, offer a short prayer, asking the Holy Spirit to create a bond of Christian friendship and collegiality between the two of you, and asking for guidance in the months and years ahead. Give the member an opportunity to offer a prayer as well; though on this first visit, do not press the point. There will be many other opportunities to share in prayer, and every other aspect of Christian discipleship. For with this visit, your relationship has only just begun.

AN INTENSIVE FIRST FEW WEEKS

This first round of visits to your members' homes will take you several weeks, and possibly several months. You will have fifteen to twenty persons in your class, and by the time you have scheduled visits and re-scheduled when conflicts have arisen, you will find yourself involved in a very intensive introductory phase of your work. This pace will not last. In fact, it *should* not last, because the relationship you have with your class members is going to be very long-term. It must be allowed to develop gradually, and this is the only time you will be working at this level of intensity.

Allow plenty of time between visits, and try not to fit more than two into one evening. The time limit of fifty minutes helps with scheduling, of course; but there is also your own energy and concentration to consider. As you will quickly discover, relating to people you do not know well is very hard work. While you should not allow this opening round of visits to be too prolonged, neither should you rush it. Let each visit be the foundation of a relationship for the months and years ahead.

WHAT NOT TO DO WITH YOUR CLASS

Once the initial visits are completed, you will find that each member's discipleship requires your leadership in different areas and in different ways. In order for this to happen naturally and straightforwardly, there are three things you should not do:

1. DO NOT OVERLOAD YOUR MEMBERS

Once you have explained the General Rule of Discipleship, it will become clear in which areas each of your members needs to grow. But if you press them too hard, and confront them with more than they are ready to attempt—or worse, if you offer unrealistic comparisons with what others are doing—you will overload them with impossible goals and standards.

The best way to avoid this is to keep reminding yourself what happens week by week in your own covenant discipleship group. It may be that some of your class members are in covenant discipleship groups as well; but most will not be, for reasons we have discussed at several points throughout this and the two companion volumes. The discipline of weekly accountability is something unfamiliar to them—just as it was once unfamiliar to you. You must therefore remember your own strength, so to speak. Your covenant discipleship group is making you a much more seasoned disciple than you once were, but you are now relating to other church members who are still where you used to be. Don't expect too much of your class members too soon.

2. DO NOT TALK ABOUT OTHER CLASS MEMBERS

You will obviously be careful not to break the confidentiality of your relationship with each class member. But during these early weeks and months, you should go further, and avoid sharing anything at all about other members, even casual information. The only exception should be the names and addresses of the other members (see below, p. 147).

This total lack of reference to other members may seem to be taking things too far. After all, is not everyone in your class a member of the congregation, and would it not be natural to make passing references to them, as friends frequently do? Indeed, you may find your class members doing this as you talk. But there is a good reason for a "blanket of security." When your members realize that you do not talk at all about any of the other members in your class, not even about ordinary day-to-day things, they will know that they are not a subject of your conversation either. This will encourage them to extend you their trust, and will gain their acceptance of your leadership more quickly.

In the weeks and months ahead, but most especially during these early weeks, your relationship with each member is essentially one-on-one. You are the leader of a class that is a pastoral subdivision of the congregation, consisting of a number of church members. Your class is not a group, and it does not have the identity of a group. Whatever may happen with other small groups in the congregation, and whatever is being done with class meetings in other Methodist traditions, the only common denominator of your class at this stage is you, the class leader. They will accept this relationship with you far more readily than with a group.

3. DO NOT ATTEMPT TO CONVENE YOUR CLASS

By the same token, you should not attempt to convene your class as a group. To repeat the point we made in the Introduction (above, p. xvii), the recovery of the office of class leader in The United Methodist Church is not being linked to a revitalization of class meetings for all church members—at least, not yet. The reasons for this have been explained in Chapter 4 above, and also in Part 3 of the companion volume, *Forming Christian Disciples*. Your members have not been asked to attend class meetings. They have rather been asked to accept you as their class leader.

This is not to say that your class should never get together. Someone may suggest a discussion on an issue of common concern in their discipleship, or to work together on a particular service project. There may even be the desire to have a social evening, at Christmas perhaps. But it will be important for these suggestions to surface spontaneously from the members themselves, rather than from you. There are already plenty of church meetings for everyone to attend; and if you initiate yet another meeting, you will have the burden of organizing it and making it worthwhile. If your class does indicate a desire to get together, let the members make the suggestion, not you.

AT EASE AND ALERT

In Chapter 1 we suggested that the kind of leadership most needed in the church today is leadership by example—people who will show others what it means to be a faithful Christian disciple, and thus lead them in the same walk with Christ. As you begin the real business of leading your class, this means two things: you can be at ease, but you must also be alert.

1. AT EASE

You can be relaxed in that you do not have to worry about your qualifications or expertise in class leading. You need only to continue your own walk with Christ and allow your class members to follow your example. You will of course be in a covenant discipleship group, where you hold yourself accountable week by week, and this in itself will be the best example of all. As we have stressed, Christian discipleship is not a matter of accomplishment, but of intent. It is not whether we succeed in our obedience to Christ, but whether we *desire* to follow his teachings.

This desire will be very evident to your class members as they learn of your covenant accountability, and the ways in which this simple but exacting procedure helps you in your discipleship week by week. You will find them asking you about your group— whether it makes you feel inferior when you have to admit your shortcomings, whether your group ever becomes mechanical and legalistic, and many other questions (see Chapter 7 of the companion volume, *Covenant Discipleship*). If any of your members become really interested in covenant discipleship, be sure to suggest that they visit a group for several weeks, to see if they would like to join. You can assure them that membership in a group does not require them to become a class leader, and they will not be pressured to join. Their interest in your own weekly accountability, however, may indicate that they are ready to take this step in their Christian pilgrimage, and you should give them every opportunity to take it.

2. ALERT

While your covenant discipleship group gives you the headway to relax in your leadership, it does not mean that you can be careless. You need to be alert as well as at ease, because your members are going to look to you as a role model much sooner than you think. We have been at pains to stress that being a class leader does not make you an expert in the Christian life, and that your leadership is at a very basic level. But you are a leader nonetheless. Just as you have to be much more careful to follow the instruction book when you are showing a teenage son or daughter how to drive, and scrupulous about safety when you are teaching small children to swim, so you must be alert about your own discipleship when you are helping other people with theirs. You are going to be under some scrutiny.

Once again, the importance of belonging to a covenant discipleship group becomes self-evident. Since you hold yourself accountable each week, you need not be unduly concerned about this aspect of your leadership. You need to be alert, however, because in the same way that children need the authority of parents against which to develop their own identity, so your class members will need your leadership as something to "grow against."

REACTIVE RESISTANCE

You will encounter this need among your class members in what can best be described as "reactive resistance." It is reactive in that your members are now experiencing an intentional effort to help them grow in their discipleship, and to some extent their reaction will be against your efforts to guide them. But much more, it will be a reaction to the increasing exposure they have to God's grace as a result of the the methodical application of the General Rule of Discipleship. And almost always, the reaction will be one of resistance.

There is much about this that you will recognize from your own resistance to God's gracious initiatives, because it is a normative pattern for sinful human beings. Indeed, the first place to turn for an explanation is the Bible, beginning with the Old Testament. In an article that should be required reading for all pastoral leaders, clergy and lay, Walter Brueggemann has described how the Hebrews learned what it meant to be in covenant with a God who was not a "passive silent upholder," but an "active agent" on their behalf. They came to understand that the essential question of human existence was not how to find God, but how to respond to the God who was looking for them. They were in covenant with a God who wanted, indeed demanded, regular conversation.[106]

IN COVENANT WITH AN ACTIVE GOD

In response to this covenant-making God, Brueggemann explains, the people of Israel determined that there were three faithful human actions: to hope ("to function each day trusting that God's promises and purposes will not fail"); to listen ("to concede that we are subject to Another who legitimately addresses us by name and tells us who we are"); and obedient answering ("the doing of justice and righteousness, loyalty and graciousness").

Since this is the God who was also in Christ, the same question confronts the pastoral leaders of the church, namely, "how persons who are hopeless, persistent speakers, and faithless listeners can be brought to faithful covenanting." Put another way, how can sinful people, who instinctively resist God, be taught how not to resist God's grace? Brueggemann further explains that the Hebrews effected this transition in three ways: by raging and protesting against God ("Israel dared to believe that sometimes protest . . . is more fitting than submission"); by grieving before God ("Israel was not reticent to speak about loss, hurt, betrayal, fear, threat, anxiety"); and by praise ("the most faithful act of getting one's mind off one's self and fully on to this One who is the real subject of our lives").[107]

These actions are no less appropriate for Christian disciples today. As you endeavor to lead your class toward faithful response to God—in hope, in listening, and in obedient answering—you will encounter reactive resistance. Not only should you expect this: you should allow it to happen, and even encourage it. From time to time, your members will rage and protest against God. Let them voice their anger and resentment at God for disturbing their lives. They will grieve before God. Help them to lament the misfortunes they feel that life has dealt them. For with all of this vented, they will eventually turn to praise God; and this you can likewise help them to do. Indeed, it will be one of the most rewarding aspects of your work as a class leader to empathize with the rage, the protest, and the grief of your class members as they resist God's grace, and then share in their praise as they come to accept the easy yoke and the light burden of obedience to Jesus Christ (Matt. 11:30).

JOYFUL SURRENDER

The more you encounter this reactive resistance in your members, the more you will be reminded of your own covenant relationship with God, and the wonder you invariably experience when you surrender to God's grace. This is not a game that God plays with us, seeking to wear us down. The God who went to the cross in order to break our resistance was playing no game. The whole point of this relationship is that God is God, and we are God's creation. If there is a game at all, then the name of this game is that God must be acknowledged to be God, and we must live as God intended us to live—in the freedom of loving obedience.

Once we accept these ground rules, there is the indescribable joy and peace of surrender to God's will. We talked in Chapter 6 about those who experience this as a "new birth" (above, pp. 116-117), and those who experience it more gradually. The further reality is that the cycle of resistance and surrender continues throughout our Christian lives. You know this from your own discipleship, and you will find it in the discipleship of your members. As their class leader, you will find yourself time and again helping them to surrender to God's grace. You will quickly learn to recognize the signs of the struggle—the rage, the protest, the grief—and you will learn to hold your ground against their resistance. They will finally surrender each time, as you yourself surrender, in joy and in peace.

As in so many of his hymns, Charles Wesley gives us the words to express our inmost thoughts and feelings:

> The godly grief, the pleasing smart,
> The meltings of a broken heart;
> The tears that tell your sins forgiven;
> The sighs that waft your souls to heaven;
>
> The guiltless shame, the sweet distress,
> Th' unutterable tenderness;
> The genuine, meek humility;
> The wonder, 'Why such love to me?'
>
> Th'o'erwhelming power of saving grace,
> The sight that veils the seraph's face,
> The speechless awe that dares not move,
> And all the silent heaven of love![108]

GETTING CAUGHT IN THE CROSSFIRE

Needless to say, you will sometimes get caught in the crossfire of this vigorous dialogue with God. Your members may direct their rage and their protest toward you: "What right have you to tell me to be more regular in prayer?" "Who are you to tell me that I should be more concerned about racial injustice in our community?" Likewise they may work through their grief at your expense: "It's all very well for you to talk about faithful discipleship, but you have no idea what I have to cope with." "You talk about the cost of discipleship, but I don't see you suffering all that much for Jesus Christ. In fact, you seem to have it pretty good."

Shots like this may leave you stinging, and may even be in the form of fiery darts that pierce your armor. But you will also share with your members those times when they accept God's will in their lives, when their rage, their protest, and their grief turn to praise. To be caught in a crossfire of praise between God and one of your members who has just come through a crisis of obedience will be the most rewarding aspect of your work as a class leader. The important thing to remember is that God is an active and generative partner in all of this. There will always be something going on in the lives of your members.

A CHRIST-CENTERED RELATIONSHIP

The great advantage of Christian discipleship is that this covenant relationship with God is centered on Jesus Christ, who shapes our hope, directs our listening, and instructs us in our obedience. In this Jew of Nazareth we have a definitive role model and a sympathetic guide—against whom, by the same token, we vent our rage and our protestations, before whom we grieve, and whom we also praise and worship.

It is therefore Jesus Christ who is at the center of the General Rule of Discipleship, as the diagram on p. 130 illustrates. You will be familiar with this Rule in your covenant discipleship group, but it is now your task as class leader to extend its guidelines to the members of your class. As you do so, you will find the cycle of reactive resistance and joyful surrender repeated many times. But it will not be an aimless cycle. There will be growth and, with time, the maturity of a seasoned obedience.

BECOMING INFORMED ABOUT YOUR CONGREGATION

During the first visit with your members, you will have introduced them to the General Rule of Discipleship, and left them a copy so that they can review their discipleship according to its guidelines. Your next contact will therefore help to focus each member on where she or he feels the need for guidance and information. Before doing this, inform yourself about the ministry and mission of your congregation in light of the General Rule. This does not mean you have to become a mine of information, but you will find it helpful to have more than a vague idea about the programs and activities that are available.

There is no priority implied in the sequence of the General Rule, and thus the random order of the following questions, which you may find helpful as you gather your information:

1. ACTS OF WORSHIP

When are the regular times of worship in the congregation? If there is more than one service on a Sunday, are there differences of style and content? How often is the sacrament of Holy Communion available? What opportunities are there for assisting in worship services? For helping to design worship services? How are prayer concerns handled?

2. ACTS OF COMPASSION

What is the congregation doing in terms of "hands-on" ministry: For church members in need? For needy or disadvantaged persons in the community at large? Around the world? How do church members get involved in these ministries? How do they start new ones? What procedures are in place to avoid duplication or crossed wires, both within the congregation and in the wider community?

3. ACTS OF DEVOTION

How does your congregation help members with their devotional life? Which resources are recommended, and how many of them provided? Are there prayer groups, Bible study groups, discussion groups, reflection groups? What is the Sunday school curriculum? Who teaches it, how often, and when? To what extent is spirituality integral to congregational life and work?

4. ACTS OF JUSTICE

Where is the congregation involved in issues of justice, both individual and social? Are there groups or persons at work to determine what these issues are, and where a Christian presence is needed? How is the congregation made aware of the global mission of the church? Are there specific projects under way that provide opportunities for direct action?

You need not feel tied to these questions, of course, nor should you feel limited by them. Hopefully they demonstrate that if you are going to ask your members to apply the General Rule of Discipleship to their lives, you cannot leave them with only abstract ideas. As we noted earlier in the chapter, avoid overwhelming them with things to do; but by the same token, do not leave them empty-handed when they ask for guidance. Much of your work as a class leader will be to direct them into more concrete forms of discipleship, and you will find programs and ministries for this already in place in your congregation, probably far more than you imagined. As a class leader you can help your members take advantage of these opportunities.

FURTHER CONTACT WITH YOUR MEMBERS

Once you are informed about the ministries and programs of your congregation, you can begin the second round of contacts with your members. These do not need to be as structured as the initial visits. You can take advantage of all the informal meetings you have in the life and work of the church, and you can make good use of the telephone. Nor should you forget the impact of a short letter or a greeting card. A telephone call, or even a personal conversation, leaves only a memory; but a written message can be read and reread many times.

This is not to say that you should cease to make visits to each member's home. On the contrary, these can become a regular feature of your leadership—not rigidly scheduled, but something you can both look forward to as a time of sharing and accountability for the General Rule. A suggested minimum for this is once each quarter, though you and your members can agree on a frequency you find mutually helpful. You will not only find these times together important for the growth of your members' discipleship;

you will also find new ideas emerging for the congregation as you ask them to apply the General Rule to their lives. Focusing their discipleship will be a creative work of grace for everyone.

APPLYING THE GENERAL RULE

As a final preparation for extending the General Rule to your class, you may wish to refer to Chapter 5 of the companion volume, *Covenant Discipleship*, in which the components of the Rule are discussed in some detail. You will be familiar with these as a framework for your group covenant, but it can be helpful to have them fresh in your mind as you begin to explain them to your members.

1. WITNESSING TO JESUS CHRIST IN THE WORLD

This first component of the General Rule may well present some difficulty, in that witnessing to Jesus Christ is often identified in North America with an assertive and even aggressive form of evangelism that leaves people uncomfortable. As a class leader, you need to make clear to your members that this is not what is implied by "witnessing to Jesus Christ." Moreover, this image of evangelism is a generalization that does not stand up to examination in the church at large. There may be some evangelists who have acted irresponsibly in our day and age; but there are countless others who are engaged in vitally important work for Jesus Christ, and without whom the preparation of the world for the coming reign of God would be seriously impaired.

To witness to Jesus Christ in the world simply means to declare our identity as Christian disciples. It is the one thing that ultimately distinguishes the Christian, not only from adherents to other religious faiths, but also from other practitioners of good works. There are many non-Christians in the world who follow the teachings of Jesus, because many of his teachings are not unique to Christianity. Moreover, Jesus made clear that such persons would be honored by him for their good works (Matt.25:40). But to declare that the Christ who has died is risen, and will come again, as sovereign of the world—that is uniquely Christian.

The members of your class will have declared these beliefs when they joined the congregation. Now you can help them to see the importance of declaring them in the world: in the places where they work, in the neighborhoods where they live, to their families, to their friends; indeed, to as many as possible, as often as possible, in as many ways as possible. They do not need special training for this. They just need to be reminded how important it is to do it. That is why it is in the General Rule. Each time you meet with them, therefore, ask them to tell you about the most recent opportunity they have had to declare their identity as a disciple of Jesus Christ—and whether or not they did.

2. ACTS OF COMPASSION

This component of the General Rule is likely to present less difficulty for your class. For one thing, there are few people who will not readily help those who are in need. There may be large systemic problems in North American society, but there are countless deeds of kindness every day throughout the country, many of them done by Christians as a matter of course. You may well have members of your class who think it unnecessary or even offensive to be held accountable for what they are already doing, and doing instinctively.

If you have members already committed to ministries of compassion, do not make the mistake of suggesting improvements. Rather, affirm them for fulfilling this part of the General Rule, and ask if they can use some help. There may be other members of the class, or members of other classes, who need to be pointed in this direction. One question you might raise with such members in due course, however, is whether their acts of compassion are causing them to neglect other dimensions of the Rule: their devotional life, or their concern for God's justice. Sometimes a person can get so involved in helping needy people that he or she neglects to address the causes of their need in the first place; whereas both have equal emphasis in the General Rule.

3. ACTS OF WORSHIP

This too will present little difficulty for your class, in that weekly worship is an accepted norm for church membership. Even so, the average attendance at United Methodist congregations on any given Sunday is only around 30-35 percent of the membership roll, and you should therefore not neglect it as a component of the General Rule. If you have members who find it difficult to get to church, ask other class members to help out; and if the congregation does not have a ministry for Sunday morning rides, then the leaders' meeting should urge the administrative council to form one. By the same token, if there is no tape ministry in place for shut-in church members, this could be a similar recommendation.

(*Note*: the leaders' meeting and individual class leaders should function primarily as sources of information and motivation for these and other ministries. Administrative and programmatic bodies of the congregation are already in place to implement them.)

There are two further points to be made with regard to worship. The first is that a broadcast service, on television or radio, is no substitute for being part of the congregation at worship. If a class member is able to get to church, do not accept the argument that a broadcast service is just as good. It is not.

The other point concerns the sacrament of the Lord's Supper, or Holy Communion. There is still a widespread reluctance in United Methodist congregations to partake of Holy Communion as a regular means of grace. In many places it is offered only monthly, or less frequently, and there are members who will stay away on a communion Sunday even then. You have probably dealt with this issue in your covenant discipleship group, but if you still have personal questions about the significance of this sacrament, do not hesitate to bring it up at the leaders' meeting, or with your pastor. Of all the means of grace, this is the most gracious, and you have an opportunity to share the richness of its significance with your class. Be sure to do so. If there is sufficient interest on the part of your members, suggest to the leaders' meeting that a Sunday evening or midweek time-slot in congregational activities be devoted to a presentation and discussion on the theme.

4. ACTS OF JUSTICE

This part of the General Rule is likely to present your class members with more of a challenge in their discipleship, because most North American congregations today view discipleship as a predominantly personal matter. We have alluded to the reasons for this in Chapters 1 and 4, and explored it in some detail in Part 1 of *Forming Christian Disciples*. But in essence it means that the teachings of Jesus concerning God's justice in the world are rarely integrated with the basics of Christian discipleship. They are more often consigned to

ministries of "social concerns," or "social action," and are sometimes even dismissed as "radical" or "secular"—just as the teachings of Jesus about personal discipleship are sometimes regarded as
"pietistic" or "otherworldly."

It will be your task as a class leader to show your members how to
make acts of justice an integral part of their discipleship. As with
your approach to Christian witness, do not present this part of the
General Rule with a heavy hand. Be ready with practical suggestions as to how your members can become involved with God's
justice in the world. Your pastor or the church office will have plenty
of leads for you to follow; and if not, you can contact the General
Board of Church and Society.[109] Explain to your members that God's
justice is not an idealistic principle, but an active concern for those
who are downtrodden, victimized, and in need of someone to take
up their cause. Point out that Jesus began his ministry by quoting
precisely this directive from the prophet Isaiah (Luke 4:18-19), and
that he also taught us to regard everyone as our neighbor (Luke
10:36-37). Above all, aim your members toward those parts of your
community where Jesus is being dishonored through neglect of the
poor and discrimination against the weak. Remember to stress the
wording of the General Rule—that these should be *acts* of justice,
not mere rhetoric.

Once again you will be helped by your covenant discipleship
group. Acts of justice will be part of your group covenant, and
through your weekly accountability your own discipleship will include this aspect of Jesus' teachings. As you share your insights with
your class, some members will be apprehensive about getting involved in social struggles, just as you probably once were. But when
their obedience to Jesus Christ brings them into personal contact
with people who are in need, they will quickly see the need to
champion God's justice in places of civic authority. If a family is
hungry, why are they hungry? If they are on welfare, who gets most
of their welfare money, sooner or later? What was the real reason for
someone losing a job?

Your quiet persistence will help your members to grow in this area
of their discipleship. There will, of course, be the usual cycle of
reactive resistance (above, p. 136). But there will also be the joyful
surrender of obedience to the God of justice and righteousness, who
favors the widow and the orphan. With your leadership, your class
members will gain the courage to be ambassadors for Christ in every
dimension of society.

5. ACTS OF DEVOTION

This too may be a more challenging part of the General Rule for your members. A great deal is taken for granted these days when it comes to devotional activities. Prayer and Bible study are often assumed to be an integral part of everyone's discipleship—so much so that there are times when these disciplines are disdained as a distraction from the work of Christ in the world. It is therefore worth repeating a statistic that has remained remarkably consistent in the eight years we have staffed covenant discipleship at the General Board of Discipleship in Nashville. When it is asked at workshops, seminars, or conferences, how many of the participants have a regular devotional life of daily prayer, daily Bible reading, and exercise temperance in their personal lives, the response has consistently been 2 percent—one out of fifty. And these are people who are sufficiently dedicated to come to seminars and workshops!

Do not take the devotional life of your members for granted. If they have not practiced these disciplines before, suggest a devotional guide such as *The Upper Room*. If they are ready for something more searching, your pastor and your church office will have plenty of ideas and information: *Disciple* Bible Study, for example, or a readable Commentary. If you sense that a member is in need of spiritual renewal, again there are many possibilities: *Walk to Emmaus*, an adaptation of the Roman Catholic *Cursillo*, consists of an intensive weekend of spiritual guidance, with follow-up support; *Renovaré* Conferences, led by Richard Foster, are quickly becoming an established resource for evangelical spirituality. The offerings are rich and varied.[110]

6. THE GUIDANCE OF THE HOLY SPIRIT

As you guide and shape the discipleship of your members, remember that they will not be able to follow the teachings of Jesus unless they are open to the power and presence of the Holy Spirit in their lives. Your covenant discipleship group has probably wrestled with what it means to receive spiritual "promptings" and "warnings," and you will be able to share some of these insights with your members. In addition, you can consult Chapter 5 of the companion volume, *Covenant Discipleship*, and also the *Covenant Discipleship Journal*.[111]

If you need further suggestions, ask your colleagues at the leaders' meeting. Likewise, ask your pastor for a bibliography in this area. The literature now available is very extensive indeed, not least because of increased cooperation between Protestants and Roman Catholics. A book such as *Reaching Out*, by Henri Nouwen, or a Puritan classic such as *My Utmost for His Highest*, by Oswald Chambers, will quickly whet your appetite for further such reading.[112] But at the same time, do not hesitate to pass on to your class members your own experience of the Holy Spirit. That will be what ultimately authenticates your leadership—the inward witness of God's Spirit in your own discipleship, confirming the presence of God's Spirit in theirs.

CONNECTING YOUR CLASS MEMBERS

In revitalizing the office of class leader, we have stressed the need for leaders to work with class members individually, and not as a group. The reasons have been explained several times above, pp. xvii, 74, 134, but two qualifying factors should now be mentioned in conclusion.

The first is that your class need not be totally disconnected. When your members have been assigned, and you have ascertained their willingness to be in your class, prepare a list of names, addresses, and telephone numbers, including your own as leader. This can be circulated to all members, and kept accurately up to date. In this way, your class has an identity, and the members know with whom they share your leadership. The leaders' meeting should also prepare a composite listing of all classes and class leaders, to be distributed throughout the congregation at least twice a year.

The second word is more a hope than a qualification of what has been said. If the Holy Spirit should move in and through your class to draw the members into the mutual accountability of a class meeting, so that everyone shares the relationships you have formed with each member individually, may you have the discernment and the grace to let it happen. Indeed, may it one day happen to all of Methodism.

FOR REFLECTION

1. Are you clear about the office of class leader? In which areas do you need additional clarification?

2. Are you comfortable with the General Rule of Discipleship as a basic guideline for your class members?

3. Do you feel that your weekly covenant discipleship group has made you a more seasoned disciple? (p. 133)

4. Is "reactive resistance" something you experience in your discipleship? (p. 136)

5. Do you find God to be an "active agent" who demands regular conversation with you? (p. 136)

6. Have you ever "raged and protested" against God? (p. 137)

7. Are you ever "caught in the crossfire" of other people's dialogue with God? (p. 139)

8. What do you know about your congregation's ministry and mission in light of the General Rule of Discipleship?

9. Which parts of the General Rule challenge you most in your discipleship?

10. To what extent does the Holy Spirit guide you in your walk with Christ?

Conclusion

In Harmony with One Another

KNOWING WHO YOU ARE

The heading for these concluding words comes from Paul's letter to the church at Rome: "Live in harmony with one another; do not be haughty, but associate with the lowly; do not claim to be wiser than you are" (12:16). Since many of the preceding pages have been devoted to confirming your call, bolstering your confidence, and assuring you that you are in fact able to do the work of a class leader, it may seem contradictory to conclude with a warning not to get "too big for your boots."

Yet that is exactly the warning that you need, and it comes from the collective experience of all of us who have been called to pastoral leadership—to the care of souls. The progression is quite predictable, and we see it in the training of the very first disciples: First, a disbelief that we are being called at all; then a feeling of unworthiness for the task; then an unwillingness to do the task, even when we know that God has given us, and will continue to give us, the gifts and graces we need; and finally a grudging acceptance of the call, and even a sullen "Have it your way."

However, once we are embarked on the task, we begin to sense the power and presence of the Holy Spirit as our gifts and graces are utilized as never before. We begin to see that other people are looking to us for leadership, and more, that we have leadership for them. As people give us their trust, we come to know the high privilege of guiding them in the Christian life, and perhaps the supreme privilege of introducing them to Christ. The problem is that all of this can easily go to our head—at which point, we become very dangerous persons indeed.

SPIRITUAL DISCERNMENT

Of all the gifts and graces given to us for pastoral leadership, none is more powerful and penetrating than the gift of spiritual discernment. In order to help people, we are given access to their

149

inmost struggles, and quite often their inmost secrets. They will not always tell us what these struggles and secrets are; quite the contrary, they will rarely tell us at all, because much of the time they do not know themselves what is going in their hearts and lives. But we may sense what is going on; and, granted the gift of spiritual discernment, we may be disconcertingly correct. We may see how God is dealing with other persons long before they themselves realize what is happening.

A DANGEROUS GIFT

This is what makes us dangerous persons—dangerous because we have the power to know other people better than they know themselves. We can use this power to help them, nurture them, and guide them toward faithful discipleship, or we can use it to our own advantage by hoarding our insights as a form of pastoral superiority over them. If we opt for the latter, there will eventually come a time when we express this superiority, however carefully we try to hide it. And in a moment of crisis or vulnerability, we will use it to judge and condemn other persons, revealing to them things about themselves they never suspected, and which they are not at all prepared to hear—revelations that can often be quite shattering for them.

This is a grave abuse of a spiritual gift. It is not at all how the Holy Spirit deals with people, as we should know only too well from our own experience. The freedom of growth in discipleship is not only the abundance of grace, but also the purging of our sin at a pace that does not crush us. If we were to be shown all of our faults all at once, we would not survive the encounter. But God's Spirit deals with our residual sin a step at a time. Once again, Charles Wesley puts it beautifully and prayerfully:

> Open, Lord, my inward ear,
> And bid my heart rejoice!
> Bid my quiet spirit hear
> Thy comfortable voice,
> Never in the whirlwind found,
> Or where the earthquakes rock the place;
> Still and silent is the sound,
> The whisper of thy grace.

. . . . . .

Show me, as my soul can bear,
The depth of inbred sin,
All the unbelief declare,
The pride that lurks within;
Take me, whom thyself hast bought,
Bring into captivity
Every high aspiring thought
That would not stoop to thee.[113]

Since this is how the Holy Spirit deals with us, this is how we must deal with other people, not merely in our interpersonal contacts, but much more in the secrecy of our hearts. The danger does not lie in the pulling of spiritual rank; few of us are that brash, or that brave. But the harboring of spiritual superiority will quickly disempower your leadership. Don't let it.

DEAL CHARITABLY WITH YOUR MEMBERS

As you begin to exercise the true power of your class leadership, therefore, your watchword must be to deal charitably with your members. Not only will they trust you with their gifts and graces, but they will also trust you with their weaknesses. You must use this trust to help them grow in their discipleship, and in their love for Jesus Christ.

You must deal charitably with your members even when they turn on you. This does not mean that they will attack you physically. But they may well attack you intellectually or emotionally, and they are certainly going to attack you spiritually. To put it more accurately, they are going to defend themselves pastorally by going on the attack against you. The reason is that, when they realize they have made themselves vulnerable to you in areas of weakness, they may try to justify themselves by criticizing you. As we noted in Chapter 7, one of the first lessons in pastoral leadership is to weather these attacks of self-defense. They are a healthy sign of growth in the other person, and they are not motivated by vindictiveness. They are rather a symptom of Beelzebul losing yet another skirmish, or maybe a major battle. If this results in a few cuts and bruises for you, they will be honorable battle scars.

DEAL CHARITABLY WITH YOUR PASTOR

Another area in which charity must be your watchword is in dealing with your pastor. We saw in Chapter 3 how Methodism had a golden opportunity some 200 years ago to forge a creative collegiality between clergy and laity in pastoral leadership, and how that opportunity was lost. There are those who would lay the onus of this on clergy who wanted to be in charge. There are others who would say that it was due to class leaders who refused to adjust to the leadership of resident pastors, and who went off to pout. More important than apportioning retrospective blame, however, is that we learn the lesson of this part of our history, and do everything we can not to repeat the mistake.

The lesson lies in mutual acceptance of God's call. As a class leader, you will have received a call from God very similar to that of your pastor. Indeed, as we also saw in Chapter 3, many of the clergy in the new Methodist Episcopal Church were first of all class leaders. That is how they learned the care of souls. That is how they first answered their call. Moreover, there must have been many class leaders who would have liked to become itinerant preachers or circuit riders, but who had family or other responsibilities they could not, or would not, leave behind.

This similarity of call led to many tensions between pastors and class leaders; and the same tensions may well occur between you and your pastor. Having such a similar calling will make you very sensitive to her or his pastoral leadership; and when you match this with your gift of spiritual discernment, you will find yourself acutely aware of his or her limitations and weaknesses. There will be times, in fact, when it is all you can do to keep your criticisms to yourself. You will be convinced that you could do far better, given the chance.

A QUESTION OF CALLING

The point is that you *have* had the chance to become a pastor, and probably still do. The difference between you and your pastor is that he or she has taken the step of leaving other responsibilities and opportunities behind, has gone through a course of theological and pastoral training that is far more rigorous than most people imagine, and has been confirmed at many stages in this process by committees and boards, some of which are composed of laypersons such as yourself. If you feel you are a better pastoral leader than your pastor, then the question you need to ask is why you have not gone through the same process. In other words, it is a question of calling.

The way to answer this question is not to disparage your pastor's theological training. It is easy to find failings in this as in any other course of professional preparation. But just as you want a qualified surgeon when you have an appendix that needs removing, never mind what you might have said and thought about the medical profession in general, so there are times when a pastor's theological training stands you and your congregation in very good stead. The problem, as we have tried to suggest throughout this and the two companion volumes, is that pastors rarely have the opportunity to use that training in the church of today. They are too preoccupied with institutional maintenance, often at a custodial level; and in many instances they are terribly overburdened with basic pastoring that could be done just as well, if not better, by laypersons.

As a class leader, you can do much to free your pastor for the work she or he was called and trained to do. However, you will do this only if you recognize that your callings are different. Many of us could be outstanding in a number of trades or professions; but we have to make a choice in life, and we must let others make theirs. It is not a question of whether you are better at pastoral leadership than your pastor. In all probability you could be—but it is not your calling.

TRUE CHRISTIAN COLLEGIALITY

Once you have this question of calling clear, you will be able to establish a true Christian collegiality that has limitless potential for both you and your pastor. You will be able to draw on her or his theological training to expand your own knowledge and understanding of the Christian tradition. In turn, this will enable and encourage your pastor to develop theological knowledge and pastoral skills that convince you both that your callings are altogether complementary. You, your pastor, your fellow class leaders, and your class members, will discover the infinite riches of being "one body in Christ, and individually . . . members one of another" (Rom. 12:4-5).

A FINAL WORD

Let the last word come from John Wesley himself, whose pastoral instincts allowed the office of class leader to develop in the early societies, as he saw gifts and graces in the lives of men and women called to the task of forming Christian disciples. The words come from a sermon that first appeared in 1787, titled "The More Excellent Way," and they show how his own leadership of the Methodist movement had tempered his pastoral instincts into a deep wisdom:

> It is the observation of an ancient writer that there have been from the beginning two orders of Christians. The one lived an innocent life, conforming in all things not sinful to the customs and fashions of the world, doing many good works, abstaining from gross evils, and attending the ordinances of God. They endeavoured in general to have a conscience void of offence in their outward behaviour, but did not aim at any particular strictness, being in most things like their neighbours. The other sort of Christians not only abstained from all appearance of evil, were zealous of good works in every kind, and attended all the ordinances of God; but likewise used all diligence to attain the whole mind that was in Christ, and laboured to walk in every point as their beloved Master.[114]

As a class leader, you are this "other sort of Christian." You have been called to this "more excellent way." But your call is not for your own sake; it is for the sake of others, the members of your class. Lead them well. They are now in your care.

Endnotes

1. *The Book of Discipline of The United Methodist Church* (Nashville: The United Methodist Publishing House, 1988).

2. The decline of the office of class leader marked a serious weakening in the power of lay leadership. The uniting General Conference did of course give lay delegates full membership in the Annual Conference, a new privilege for members of the Methodist Episcopal Churches (*The History of American Methodism*, gen. ed. Emory Stevens Bucke, 3 vols. [Nashville: Abingdon Press, 1964], 3:532ff.) It has always been a moot point, however, just how much power that status carries. Annual conference sessions, to say nothing of delegate election, are overwhelmingly clergy-dominated.

3. See, for example, Dick Murray, *Strengthening the Adult Sunday School Class* (Nashville: Abingdon Press, 1981).

4. See Kurt W. Back, *Beyond Words: The Story of Sensitivity Training and the Encounter Movement* (Baltimore, MD: Penguin Books, 1973), p. xxi.

5. See, for example, Mary Craig, *Six Modern Martyrs* (New York: Crossroad, 1987); Olive Fleming Liefield, *Unfolding Destinies: The Untold Story of Peter Fleming and the Auca Mission* (Grand Rapids, MI: Zondervan, 1990).

6. For additional statistics, see David Lowes Watson, *The Early Methodist Class Meeting* (Nashville: Discipleship Resources, 1985), p. 131.

7. *The Works of John Wesley, Bicentennial Edition* (hereafter cited as *Wesley's Works*): *Volume 9: The Methodist Societies: History, Nature, and Design*, ed. Rupert E. Davies (Nashville: Abingdon Press, 1989), p. 69.

8. See Frank Baker, *John Wesley and the Church of England* (Nashville: Abingdon Press, 1970), pp. 304-23.

9. *Wesley's Works*, 9:333.

10. Ibid., 9:340.

11. Ibid., 9:266.

12. I have argued this point at greater length in *God Does Not Foreclose: The Universal Promise of Salvation* (Nashville: Abingdon Press, 1990), pp. 38-55.

13. See K. James Stein, *Philipp Jakob Spener: Pietist Patriarch* (Chicago, IL: Covenant Press, 1986), p. 86.

14. See Richard P., Heitzenrater, *Mirror and Memory: Reflections on Early Methodism* (Nashville: Kingswood Books, 1989), pp. 33-45.

15. *Wesley's Works: Volume 19: Journal and Diaries II (1738-1743)*, ed. W. Reginald Ward and Richard P. Heitzenrater (Nashville: Abingdon Press, 1990), p. 258.

16. *Wesley's Works*, 9:529.

17. See David Lowes Watson, "Aldersgate Street and the General Rules: The Form and the Power of Methodist Discipleship," in *Aldersgate Reconsidered*, ed. Randy L. Maddox (Nashville: Kingswood Books, 1990), pp. 33-47.

18. *Wesley's Works*, 9:262.

19. Ibid., 9:263.

20. Ibid.

21. Joseph Nightingale, *A Portraiture of Methodism* (London, 1807), p. 273. See also Watson, *Early Class Meeting*, pp. 101-2.

22. *Wesley's Works*, 9:261.

23. Ibid., 9:265.

24. Ibid.

25. *The Journal of The Rev. John Wesley, A.M.*, ed. Nehemiah Curnock. Standard Edition, 8 vols. (London: Charles H. Kelly, 1909-1916), 3:284-85. See also Watson, *Early Class Meeting*, pp. 104-8.

26. See Chapter 2 of the companion volume, *Forming Christian Disciples*.

27. *Wesley's Works*, 9:72.

28. See Frederick Herzog, *God-Walk: Liberation Shaping Dogmatics* (Maryknoll, NY: Orbis Books, 1988.

29. *Life of William Carvosso, Sixty Years a Class-Leader* (Cincinnati and New York, 2nd ed., 1835).

30. Ibid., p. 218.

31. See Robert E. Coleman, *"Nothing to Do But to Save Souls"* (Grand Rapids, MI: Francis Asbury Press, 1990). See also Robert G. Tuttle, *On Giant Shoulders: The history, role, and influence of the evangelist in the movement called Methodism* (Nashville: Discipleship Resources, 1984).

32. *Carvosso*, p. 220.

33. Ibid., pp. 261-63.

34. Ibid., p. 268.

35. Ibid., pp. 8-9.

36. Much of this section relies on Frank Baker, *From Wesley to Asbury: Studies in Early American Methodism* (Durham, NC: Duke University Press, 1976). See especially pp. 23ff., 33ff., 51ff.

37. *The Doctrines and Discipline of the Methodist Episcopal Church, in America. With Explanatory Notes by Thomas Coke and Francis Asbury (1798)*. Facsimile Edition, edited by Frederick A. Norwood. Published under the Sponsorship of The Institute for the Study of Methodism and Related Movements, Garrett-Evangelical Theological Semionary, Evanston, Illinois (Rutland, Vt.: Academy Books, 1979), p. 148.

38. *The Life of The Rev. John Emory, D.D.*, by his eldest son (New York, 1841), p. 28.

39. *Autobiography of Rev. James B. Finley; or, Pioneer Life in the West* (Cincinnati, 1855), pp. 177-79.

40. Ibid., p. 180.

41. John Miley, *Treatise on Class Meetings* (Cincinnati, 1954); L[eonidas] Rosser, *Class Meetings: Embracing their Origin, Obligation, and Benefits* (Richmond, VA, 2nd ed., 1855).

42. Rosser, p. 258.

43. Ibid., pp. 259-71.

44. For the "Rules of the Band Societies" (1738), see *Wesley's Works*, 9:77-78.

45. Ibid., 9:540.

46. Frank Baker, *John Wesley and the Church of England* (Nashville: Abingdon Press, 1970), pp. 4-5.

47. *The Letters of The Rev. John Wesley, A.M.*, ed. John Telford, 8 vols. (London: Epworth Press, 1931), 7:238.

48. Frederick A. Norwood, *The Story of American Methodism: A History of the United Methodists and Their Relations* (Nashville: Abingdon Press, 1974), p. 132.

49. See Heitzenrater, *Mirror and Memory*, pp. 189-204. See also Thomas C. Oden, *Doctrinal Standards in the Wesleyan Tradition* (Grand Rapids, MI: Francis Asbury Press, 1988), pp. 201-4.

50. *History of American Methodism*, 1:374, #23.

51. Wesley, *Letters*, 8:196.

52. These were the O'Kelly schism at the 1792 General Conference of the Methodist Episcopal Church (see Baker, *Wesley to Asbury*, pp. 133-34), and the Methodist New Connexion in England in 1797 (see *A History of The Methodist Church in Great Britain*, gen. eds. Rupert Davies, A. Raymond George, Gordon Rupp, 4 vols. [London: Epworth Press, 1965-1988], 2:288ff.).

53. Miley, *Class Leaders*, pp. 211ff.

54. Norwood, *Story of American Methodism*, p. 132.

55. David Sherman, *History of the Revision of the Discipline of the*

Methodist Episcopal Church (New York: Nelson & Phillips, 1874), pp. 127-28.

56. *History of American Methodism*, 1:583.

57. Ibid., 3:193-95.

58. Sherman, *History of the Discipline*, pp. 115-18.

59. *History of American Methodism*, 2:12-21.

60. Sydney E. Ahlstrom, *A Religious History of the American People* (New Haven: Yale University Press, 1972), pp. 668-69; Martin E. Marty, *Righteous Empire: The Protestant Experience in America* (New York: The Dial Press, 1970), pp. 119-20.

61. *History of American Methodism*, 2:22-39. See also H. Shelton Smith, *In His Image, But . . . : Racism in Southern Religion, 1780-1910* (Durham, NC: Duke University Press, 1972).

62. John Atkinson, *The Class Leader: his work and how to do it* (New York, 1882), pp. 22ff., 120ff.

63. Charles L. Goodell, *The Drillmaster of Methodism: Principles and Methods for the Class Leader and Pastor* (New York, 1902).

64. F. Herbert Skeete, "The Methodist Class Meeting as a Relevant Model for Urban Ministry" (Madison, NJ: Drew University Doctor of Ministry Project, 1975), p. 29.

65. Ibid., pp. 26, 33.

66. Ibid., p. 33.

67. Bishop H.M. Turner, *The Genius and Theory of Methodist Polity, or The Machinery of Methodism* (Nashville: AMEC Sunday School Union, 1986), p. 146.

68. Skeete, "Methodist Class Meeting," pp. 41-42.

69. "Class Leader Training Guide," St. Mark's United Methodist Church, Montclair, NJ.

70. Norman E. Thomas, "Personal Piety and Social Witness: A Case Study in Zimbabwe," *Journal of the Academy for Evangelism in Theological Education*, 1 (1985-86):65-66.

71. Ibid.

72. Gloster S. Udy, *Key to Change* (2nd ed., Sydney, 1985). See also John Mallison, *Growing Christians in Small Groups* (Sydney, Australia: Scripture Union Books; Melbourne, Australia: The Joint Board of Christian Education, 1989). See also Robert and Julia Banks, *The Home Church: Regrouping the People of God for Community and Mission* (Sutherland, Australia: Albatross Books, 1986). *Downstream*, a newsletter "for telling the stories of Christian people and groups who are reaching out to people around them," is edited by David Nash, and published by the Uniting

Church Board of Mission, P.O. Box E178, St. James 2000, Australia.

73. David Lowes Watson, *Wenn zwei oder drei in meinem Namen versammelt sind*, tr. Helmut Nausner (Zürich: Gotthelf Verlag, 1990).

74. David Chavez, "Pactos: A Manual for Local Church Ministries" (1990). For a detailed study of *base communities*, see Guillermo Cook, *The Expectation of the Poor: Latin American Basic Ecclesial Communities in Protestant Perspective* (Maryknoll: Orbis Books, 1985). See especially chapter 10 for links with early Methodism. See also Watson, *God Does Not Foreclose*, pp. 131-34.

75. Hae-Jong Kim, "Use of Class Meetings for Unifying Pastoral Ministry and for Church Growth in the Korean-American Immigrant Churches" (Madison, NJ: Drew University Doctor of Ministry Project, 1984), pp. 51-52.

76. Paul Yonggi Cho, *Successful Home Cell Groups* (South Plainfield, NJ: Bridge Publishing Company, 1981.

77. Hae-Jong Kim, "Class Meetings," p. 90.

78. Ibid., p. 101.

79. *Wesley's Works: Volume 1: Sermons I, 1-33*, ed. Albert C. Outler (Nashville: Abingdon Press, 1984), p. 104.

80. These issues are addressed in more detail in Part 1 of the companion volume, *Forming Christian Disciples* (#DR093B).

81. See George H. Gallup, Jr., *Religion in America 1990* (Princeton, NJ: Princeton Religion Research Center, 1990).

82. Stanley Hauerwas and William H. Willimon, *Resident Aliens: Life in the Christian Colony* (Nashville: Abingdon Press, 1989).

83. *Wesley's Works*, 9:67-75.

84. Lesslie Newbigin, *Foolishness to the Greeks: The Gospel and Western Culture* (Grand Rapids, MI: Wm. B. Eerdmans, 1986), p. 1.

85. See above, n.63.

86. *Book of Discipline* (1988), para.268.

87. An order for the Commissioning of Class Leaders is planned for inclusion in the forthcoming United Methodist *Book of Worship*.

88. *Wesley's Works: Volume 2: Sermons II, 34-70*, ed. Albert C. Outler (Nashville: Abingdon Press, 1985), pp. 87-89.

89. The *Journal for Covenant Discipleship*, edited by Marigene Chamberlain, has a separate page for each week of the year, designed according to the General Rule of Discipleship. This enables members to record their experiences and insights, and thus give a more meaningful account of their discipleship at their weekly

meetings. It is available from the Office of Covenant Discipleship and Christian Formation, P.O. Box 840, Nashville, TN 37202-0840.

90. Rueben P. Job and Norman Shawchuck, *A Guide to Prayer for Ministers and Other Servants* (Nashville: The Upper Room, 1983), pp. 347ff.

91. This version of the prayer, adapted from the text of 1780, can be found in *John and Charles Wesley: Selected Writings and Hymns*, ed. Frank Whaling, The Classics of Western Spirituality (New York: Paulist Press, 1981), p. 140.

92 C.K. Barrett, *The Epistle to the Romans* (New York: Harper & Row, 1957), p. 238.

93. See George G. Hunter, III, *The Contageous Congregation: Frontiers in Evangelism and Church Growth* (Nashville: Abingdon Press, 1979), pp. 45ff.

94. James W. Fowler, *Weaving the New Creation: Stages of Faith and the Public Church* (HarperSanFrancisco, 1991), pp. 99-102.

95. Ibid.

96. Ibid.

97. Ibid., pp. 94ff.

98. Ibid., pp. 102ff.

99. See, for example, Susanne Johnson, *Christian Spiritual Formation in the Church and Classroom* (Nashville: Abingdon Press, 1989).

100. *Wesley's Works: Volume 19: Journal and Diaries II (1738-1743)*, ed. W. Reginald Ward and Richard P. Heitzenrater (Nashville: Abingdon Press, 1990), pp. 153-62. See also James W. Fowler, "John Wesley's Development in Faith," in *The Future of the Methodist Theological Traditions*, ed. M. Douglas Meeks (Nashville: Abingdon Press, 1985), pp. 172-92.

101. "The Marks of the New Birth," "The Great Privilege of those that are Born of God," "The New Birth," in *Wesley's Works*, 1:415-446; 2:186-201.

102. Fowler, *Weaving the New Creation*, pp. 92-93. See also Walter Conn, *Christian Conversion: A Developmental Interpretation of Autonomy and Surrender* (New York: Paulist Press, 1986); Stephen Happel & James J. Walter, *Conversion and Discipleship: A Christian Foundation for Ethics and Doctrine* (Philadelphia: Fortress Press, 1986); Urban T. Holmes, *Turning to Christ: A Theology of Renewal and Evangelization* (New York: Seabury Press, 1981); James E. Loder, *The Transforming Moment: Understanding Convictional Experiences* (San Francisco: Harper & Row, 1981); George E. Morris, *The Mystery and Meaning of Christian Conversion* (Nashville: Discipleship Resources, 1981).

103. As in "The Scripture Way of Salvation," *Wesley's Works*, 2:163-69.

104. Ibid., 3:203-4.

105. *Book of Discipline* (1988), Para.426:15,19.

106. Walter Brueggemann, "Covenanting as Human Vocation: A Discussion of the Relation of Bible and Pastoral Care," *Interpretation* 33:2 (April 1979):115-29.

107. Ibid., pp. 121-25.

108. *Wesley's Works: Volume 7: A Collection of Hymns for the Use of the People called Methodists*, ed. Franz Hildebrandt & Oliver A. Beckerlegge, asst. James Dale (Nashville: Abingdon Press, 1990), p. 92.

109. *Christian Social Action* is published eleven times a year by the General Board of Church and Society of The United Methodist Church, and in addition to topical articles, carries information on a wide range of resources. It can be ordered from: 100 Maryland Avenue, N.E., Washington, D.C. 20002.

110. Information on *Disciple: Becoming Disciples Through Bible Study* may be obtained from The United Methodist Publishing House, P.O. Box 801, Nashville, TN 37202.

Information on *Renovare* may be obtained from P.O. Box 879, Wichita, KS 67201-0879. Richard J. Foster's books are outstanding resources in spirituality and are widely used. See especially, *Celebration of Discipline: The Path to Spiritual Growth* (San Francisco: Harper & Row, 1978; revised and expanded, 1988), and *Freedom of Simplicity* (San Francisco: Harper & Row, 1981).

Information on *Walk to Emmaus* may be obtained from The Upper Room, P.O. Box 189, Nashville, TN 37202-0189.

111. See above, n.89. Additional resources for class leaders on all aspects of the General Rule of Discipleship will be supplied in *Class Leader Bulletins*. Details can be obtained from the Office of Covenant Discipleship and Christian Formation, General Board of Discipleship, P.O. Box 840, Nashville, TN 37202-0840.

112. Henri J.M. Nouwen, *Reaching Out: The Three Movements of the Spiritual Life* (Garden City, New York: Doubleday & Company, Inc., 1975); Oswald Chambers, *My Utmost for His Highest: Selections for the Year* (New York: Dodd, Mead & Company, 1935).

113. *Wesley's Works*, 7:512-13.

114. *Wesley's Works*, 3:265.

Resources

All of the following are available from: **Discipleship Resources, P.O. Box 189, Nashville, TN 37202-0189•(615)340-7284.**

Covenant Discipleship: Christian Formation through Mutual Accountability by David Lowes Watson.

This new manual advances the guidelines for covenant discipleship groups by incorporating learnings of the past decade from groups in the United States and around the world. **(#DR091B)**

Class Leaders: Recovering a Tradition by David Lowes Watson.

Taking the later Methodist class meeting as a model, this book shows how class leaders can foster the discipleship of a pastoral subdivision of the congregation. **(#DR092B)**

Forming Christian Disciples: The Role of Covenant Discipleship and Class Leaders in the Congregation by David Lowes Watson.

This third volume gives the procedures for introducing and sustaining covenant discipleship groups, and explains the role of class leaders in the congregation. **(#DR093B)**

These three books are available individually or as a set: the *Covenant Discipleship Trilogy.* **(#M302P)**

Covenants on Campus: Covenant Discipleship Groups for College and University Students by Kim Hauenstein-Mallet and Kenda Creasy Dean.

Written especially for campus ministers, college-town church leaders, and college students, this book explains the values of shared Christian discipleship according to biblical principles. **(#DR099B)**

Branch Groups: Covenant Discipleship for Youth by Lisa Grant.

An adaptation of the early Methodist class meeting for the youth of today, branch groups enable young people to practice the basics of discipleship in covenant with one another. **(#DR067B)**

The Early Methodist Class Meeting: Its Origins and Significance by David Lowes Watson. Foreword by Albert C. Outler.

This volume provides the historical background of the early class meeting, including a theological assessment of its place in Wesley's leadership of the Methodist movement. **(#DR017B)**

Wesley Speaks on Christian Vocation by Paul Wesley Chilcote.

Using Wesley's own writings as a source of inspiration, Chilcote addresses the deep vocational questions that shape the life of the faithful Christian disciple. **(#DR041B)**

Discípulos Responsables por David Lowes Watson. Prólogo por Mortimer Arias.

Este libro presenta una excelente base para la formación, desarrollo, y acción de grupos de discípulos responsables en nuestra iglesia. **(#F023B)**

Discovering the Modern Methodists

This video resource on two cassettes features David Lowes Watson in four presentations:
* The Need for Muscle in the Church
* The Dynamics of Discipleship
* The Early Methodist Class Meeting
* Covenant Discipleship Groups

Each presentation is 20 minutes long, with an accompanying leader's guide for a further 30 minutes of discussion. **(#M301VC)**

Christian Formation Binder

This vinyl three-ring binder is designed to hold copies of the *Covenant Discipleship Quarterly,* the *Journal for Covenant Discipleship,* and resources and materials for the use of class leaders in their work. **(#M303M)**

Christian Formation Brochure

Copies of this brochure are available for distribution in congregations and other settings, and may be purchased in multiples of 100. **(#M299L)**

Covenant Discipleship Quarterly

Available in English and Spanish, the *Quarterly* is an important supplement to the handbook, *Covenant Discipleship.* It features articles about Christian discipleship in different contexts, and reports from covenant discipleship groups around the world.

Journal for Covenant Discipleship

The *Journal,* with a separate page for each week of the year, provides a place for group members to record their experiences and insights, enabling them to give a more meaningful account of their discipleship at their weekly meetings.

Both the *Quarterly* and the *Journal* can be ordered from the **Office of Covenant Discipleship and Christian Formation, General Board of Discipleship, P.O. Box 840, Nashville, TN 37202-0840. (615) 340-7010.**

NOTES

NOTES

NOTES

NOTES

NOTES

NOTES